Explore the Jewish holidays ▮▮▮▮ ...er understanding of your o▮

This easy-to-understand introduction take ▮▮▮ ▮▮ral and spiritual significance of the major Jewis▮ ▮▮ you to discover how understanding each of them can enrich your own spiritual life.

Written especially for Christians, this book explores the pivotal experiences that inspired the framework for Jewish sacred time and their roles in modern Jewish spiritual life. Whether you are involved in an interfaith relationship with a Jewish person, interested in learning more about the tradition from which Christianity emerged or looking to deepen your own spiritual life through greater understanding of Jewish tradition, you will find that this introduction provides the background you need in a concise, accessible way.

"Does Christians and Christian-Jewish dialogue a great service. With straightforward explanations, invites the reader to 'walk the walk' with Judaism and find in such a pilgrimage a deeper insight into one's own beliefs. A valuable resource to promote intelligent dialogue between Christians and Jews."
— **David L. Coppola,** PhD, associate executive director, Center for Christian-Jewish Understanding, Sacred Heart University

ALSO AVAILABLE IN THIS SERIES

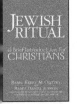

by TAMAR FRANKIEL, PhD
Demystifies the world of Kabbalah and shows that it is not only for Jewish scholars, but for anyone interested in this mystical tradition.
5½ x 8½, 208 pp, Quality Paperback Original
ISBN 978-1-58023-303-3

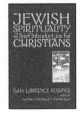

by RABBI LAWRENCE KUSHNER
Reveals to Christians the essence of Judaism through Talmud, midrash and mystical and biblical stories.
5½ x 8½, 112 pp, Quality Paperback Original
ISBN 978-1-58023-150-3

by RABBI KERRY M. OLITZKY AND RABBI DANIEL JUDSON
A look at the historical meaning and contemporary use of ten Jewish rituals including Observing the Sabbath, Keeping Kosher, Studying Torah, Prayers and Blessings and more.
5½ x 8½, 144 pp, Quality Paperback Original
ISBN 978-1-58023-210-4

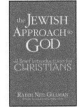

by RABBI NEIL GILLMAN
Guides you through the different ways the Jewish people have related to God, how each originated and what each may mean for Christians' understanding of their own faith.
5½ x 8½, 192 pp, Quality Paperback Original
ISBN 978-1-58023-190-9

Rabbi Kerry M. Olitzky, executive director of the Jewish Outreach Institute, is coeditor of *The Rituals and Practices of Jewish Life: A Handbook for Personal Spiritual Renewal* and *Jewish Men Pray: Words of Yearning, Praise, Petition, Gratitude and Wonder from Traditional and Contemporary Sources;* coauthor of *Jewish Ritual: A Brief Introduction for Christians;* and author of *Introducing My Faith and My Community: The Jewish Outreach Institute Guide for the Christian in a Jewish Interfaith Relationship* (all Jewish Lights), as well as many inspiring books that bring the Jewish wisdom tradition into everyday life.

Rabbi Daniel Judson, director of professional development and placement of the rabbinical school at Hebrew Union College, is coeditor of *The Rituals and Practices of a Jewish Life: A Handbook for Personal Spiritual Renewal;* and coauthor of *The Jewish Pregnancy Book: A Resource for the Soul, Body and Mind during Pregnancy, Birth and the First Three Months;* and *Jewish Ritual: A Brief Introduction for Christians* (all Jewish Lights). He is a frequent guest speaker at both Jewish and Christian congregations.

"Demystifies Jewish holidays without dumbing-down.... Will make Christian devotees with Jewish friends and partners feel more confident in participating in religious celebrations together."
—**Rev. Molly Phinney Baskette,** MDiv, coauthor, *Remembering My Grandparent: A Kid's Own Grief Workbook in the Christian Tradition*

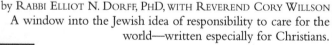

JEWISH HOLIDAYS

A Brief Introduction for CHRISTIANS

RABBI KERRY M. OLITZKY
AND RABBI DANIEL JUDSON

For People of All Faiths, All Backgrounds
JEWISH LIGHTS Publishing

Jewish Holidays:
A Brief Introduction for Christians

2014 Third Printing

Some of the material in this book is excerpted from *Introducing My Faith and My Community: The Jewish Outreach Institute Guide for the Christian in a Jewish Interfaith Relationship*, by Kerry M. Olitzky, Jewish Lights Publishing, Woodstock, Vermont © 2004; and from *The Rituals and Practices of a Jewish Life: A Handbook for Personal Spiritual Renewal*, edited by Kerry M. Olitzky and Daniel Judson, Jewish Lights Publishing, Woodstock, Vermont © 2002.

Library of Congress Cataloging-in-Publication Data
Olitzky, Kerry M.
  Jewish holidays : a brief introduction for Christians / Kerry M. Olitzky and Daniel Judson.
      p. cm.
  Includes bibliographical references.
  ISBN-13: 978-1-58023-302-6 (quality pbk.)
  ISBN-10: 1-58023-302-3 (quality pbk.)
  1. Fasts and feasts—Judaism. I. Judson, Daniel. II. Title.
  BM690.O45 2006
  296.4'3—dc22
                                                        2006026314
  ISBN 978-1-58023-547-1 (eBook)

Manufactured in the United States of America

For People of All Faiths, All Backgrounds
Published by Jewish Lights Publishing
www.jewishlights.com

ISBN 978-1-68336-143-5 (hc)

For Sheryl, my life's partner and soul companion, who continues to teach our growing family and so many others the real lessons of the Jewish holidays by transforming our home into a celebration.

—KO

And for Naftali and Maayan, with great love, and the hope that as they grow they will continue to be entranced by the holidays.

—DJ

The Judaism for Christians Series

The Jewish Approach to God
A Brief Introduction for Christians
by Rabbi Neil Gillman

The Jewish Approach to Repairing the World (*Tikkun Olam*)
A Brief Introduction for Christians
By Rabbi Elliot N. Dorff, PhD, with Rev. Cory Willson

The Jewish Connection to Israel, the Promised Land
A Brief Introduction for Christians
by Rabbi Eugene Korn, PhD

Jewish Holidays
A Brief Introduction for Christians
by Rabbi Kerry M. Olitzky and Rabbi Daniel Judson

Jewish Ritual
A Brief Introduction for Christians
by Rabbi Kerry M. Olitzky and Rabbi Daniel Judson

Jewish Spirituality
A Brief Introduction for Christians
by Rabbi Lawrence Kushner

Kabbalah
A Brief Introduction for Christians
by Tamar Frankiel, PhD

CONTENTS

Acknowledgments

This book emerged as a response to an articulated request by many Christians, particularly those who are in interfaith relationships—or their family members—and those who read *Jewish Ritual: A Brief Introduction for Christians* (Woodstock, Vt.: Jewish Lights Publishing). They wanted to know more about the Jewish holidays because they animate Jewish culture and the Jewish people. We are grateful to all those who made this suggestion.

There are many people we would like to thank, especially those at Jewish Lights Publishing, who continue to believe in us and in what we do. They make it possible for our words to take on a life beyond the fleeting moments in which they are spoken. And they bring these words to people in far-flung places so that they might hear what we have to say more readily and certainly more clearly. In particular we would like to mention Emily Wichland and Jessica Swift, whose insightful edits are any author's best companions; Kate Treworgy, who works hard to make sure that the book is seen by those who need it most; and finally, and most importantly, Stuart and Antoinette Matlins, our publishers, who constantly turn the dreams of the Jewish people into reality—only to dream once again.

We would also like to thank the many people involved in the Jewish Outreach Institute who work indefatigably to make the Jewish community more inclusive and welcoming.

We would also like to thank Dr. David Coppola of the Center for Jewish-Christian Understanding at Sacred Heart University for his help in preparing this manuscript. And a special thanks goes to all those who have enriched our lives by celebrating the Jewish holidays with us—we feel blessed and uplifted.

Rabbi Daniel Judson
Rabbi Kerry ("Shia") Olitzky

INTRODUCTION

We wrote this book because there seems to be a growing number of Christians who are interested in learning about Judaism. Some of you may have picked up this book because of a relationship with a Jewish person—someone in your family or maybe a fiancée. Others may wish to deepen an understanding of your own Christian roots. In either case, to learn about Judaism means to learn about the Jewish holidays. While there are daily rituals in Judaism that are profound and beautiful, it is the holidays that provide the peak experiences of Jewish life. Hearing the blare of a ram's horn on the Jewish New Year, seeing the family gathered around the table for the Passover meal, dancing with the Torah on Simchat Torah (the day of rejoicing with the Torah)—these are the moments that speak deeply to the Jewish soul and animate Judaism with color and with life.

This book is written directly for a Christian audience. We presume the reader is not familiar with Jewish practice and nomenclature, and we also help the Christian reader by citing Christian practices that might be analogous to those covered here. Also, there are some resources at the back of the book to aid in understanding Judaism. There is a basic explanation of the four major denominations that contemporary Judaism is divided into—Orthodox, Conservative, Reform, and Reconstructionist—and there is a calendar that shows when each of the Jewish holidays mentioned in this book occurs on the secular calendar.

But we wrote this book from a deeply Jewish perspective, as people who love Judaism, mark the Jewish holidays, and want to share that sense with Christians who might be interested. So when we use the term *we*, we are generally referring to us, as authors, reflecting the practice of the Jewish people.

As rabbis, we have liberally taken advantage of a variety of sources to support our work. These may include the Hebrew Bible (sometimes referred to as the "Written Law") and the Talmud (often called the "Oral Law"), and the prayer book. In each case, the translations are our own. In the case of biblical references, these are taken from the Hebrew Bible. As a result, you may find the citations slightly different from your own copy of the Bible.

Chapters one through eight of this book cover one particular holiday. We discuss the holiday's origins, historical development, customs, symbols, and prayers. At the end of each chapter, we have tried to discern parallels in the Christian tradition. Some of those parallels have actual connections, like Easter and Passover, while for other holidays we have made a thematic connection. Chapter nine introduces you to five minor holidays.

Chapter ten slightly differs from the format used to discuss the holidays in other chapters. This is because the topic, Shabbat (or the Sabbath), *is* different from the other holidays. First, Shabbat is observed weekly rather than annually. In addition, Shabbat can be both deeply personal and observed in a very individualized way, and it can be extremely ritualized with a variety of rules regarding behavior and practices—it all depends on who is celebrating Shabbat. It is not to say that the annual holidays can only be observed one way—that is surely not the case—it is, quite simply, that Shabbat is different from any other holiday in the Jewish calendar.

The book begins with the Jewish New Year, Rosh Hashanah, which is also the first of two holidays collectively known as the "High Holidays" or the "High Holy Days." We then cover each major holiday sequentially throughout the year. Most of the holidays mentioned in this book have their origins in the Bible. However, as you will quickly see, what the Bible says about the holiday does not always correlate to how the holiday developed over time. In the Bible, a number of holidays have agricultural contexts. The holiday of Sukkot, for example, celebrates the fall harvest. Nevertheless, as the holiday evolved over time and as Jews became less connected to the agricultural cycle, substantial additional themes emerged to explain why we celebrate the holiday. In the final chapter we cover a few minor holidays that have developed only in the past sixty years, such as the day to remember the Holocaust or to celebrate Israel's independence.

Each of the holidays mentioned in this book has both a home and a synagogue component, although the balance between them differs dramatically. For example, Yom Kippur, the holiest day of the year, is primarily observed in the synagogue, but there is a home meal that precedes the holiday (see chapter 2). Passover, on the other hand, is primarily observed in the home with a seder meal (see chapter 7), but also has a synagogue component. The home celebrations are often cited as one of the most appealing aspects of the Jewish holidays; they are a time for family to be together and celebrate our blessings.

One major theme which repeats itself in this book concerns Jewish history. For almost a millennium, the center of Jewish worship was the Temple in Jerusalem. The Temple was first destroyed in 586 BCE but was rebuilt a few generations later. The second Temple was destroyed by the Romans in 70 CE. This was a radical moment in Jewish history because the entire focus of Jewish life changed. When the Temple stood, the central practice of Judaism was sacrifice. After the Temple fell, prayer fully replaced sacrifice as the central religious act. Jewish holidays dramatically changed as well. While the Temple was standing, all the holidays included sacrifices at the Temple. Following the destruction of the Temple, each holiday was recast. Prayers and rituals were added to celebrate the holiday in a post-Temple world.

This flexibility in adapting to dramatically changed circumstances is fundamental to Jewish life. It has enabled Judaism to remain vibrant through thousands of years in places all over the world. Judaism survived the destruction of its central worship place, and it has survived many attempts at annihilation by people motivated by hate and anti-Semitism. The Jewish holidays played a crucial part in that survival. They provided generations with meaning and joy in a chaotic world.

HOW DO THE HOLIDAYS FIT TOGETHER?

Although we treat each holiday individually in this book, it is important to say a few words about the overarching threads that tie the holidays together. Dealing with holidays individually— without the benefit of a conceptual framework—is like looking at a building through peepholes drilled into a construction fence. The holes might help us get a good view of certain sections of the building, but we aren't able to see the structure as a whole. Nor are we able to see the building in the context of an entire neighborhood. So too, if we just examine one holiday we may miss the whole "neighborhood" of Judaism. Looking at the overall structure of the Jewish holidays, we see that the structure embodies significant Jewish values.

Although the High Holidays—Rosh Hashanah, the Jewish New Year, and Yom Kippur, the Day of Atonement— attract the most people to synagogues for festival services, the center of the Jewish calendar is actually Pesach, Passover. Passover is the springtime festival of freedom, which provides us with the religious foundation for the entire year and on which other holidays are built. Passover recalls the formative experience of the Jewish people, when the ancient Israelites evolved from a disparate collection of slaves in Egypt to become a united people. Thus, Passover is also about the acquisition of historical memory: a sense that those of us alive today were slaves in Egypt long ago, and that each one of us experienced the freedom from that slavery. It is probably not coincidental, therefore, that Pesach is the holiday that is observed in one form or another by more Jews in North America than any other, including Hanukkah.

As a people, Jews are nothing without this memory. It is the chief educational goal of the Passover seder meal to provide a connection to these memories. It also helps to explain why Jewish people feel a special kinship with one another because of this shared historical experience.

Each holiday in some way builds on this initial story of the Exodus from Egypt. The holiday of Shavuot, for example, celebrates the giving of the Torah at Mount Sinai, which the Bible says took place as the Jews journeyed out of Egypt and away from slavery. Judaism understands the connection between Passover and Shavuot to mean that the Israelites were freed from Egypt not simply to enjoy their freedom, but were freed to observe the words of the Torah.

On Sukkot, we build small huts in remembrance of the huts the Israelites lived in when they journeyed from Egypt. The huts remind us of our own fragility and of our deep connection with nature. Sukkot then adds to the foundation of the Exodus story, by reminding us that even as we experience freedom, we rely on God for crops to grow and for our shelter to remain stable.

Sukkot, Shavuot, and Passover are the three Jewish holidays called the pilgrimage festivals (so named because when the Temple stood, Jews were required to journey to Jerusalem for their observance). Pilgrimage may be an apt metaphor for the Jewish holidays. The Jewish people are directed to walk—and continue—the journey of our ancestors. We have to be there at every step along the journey, stopping to participate in its pivotal events in order to understand them fully. As these core holiday values develop, they make room for new holidays (like Yom Hashoah/Holocaust Remembrance Day and Yom Ha'atzmaut/Israel Independence Day) and the further articulation of Jewish values.

Our sense of the Jewish holiday cycle is that it methodically, systematically brings into focus the ultimate dimension of living in relationship with God. The holidays frame the covenantal relationship that should infuse every facet of our lives. The rituals themselves shed light on this relationship by giving us concrete forms for Jewish belief, adjusted over time by community custom and the influence of historical events. Holidays accomplish this task in several ways.

First, they articulate God's constant message to us: it is a message of hope and optimism shaped by messianism, reminding us along the way of what is possible, that we are not—and never will be—alone. Second, the holidays provide a spiritual road map for living. The totality of our lives cannot be a series of peak experiences. Thus, the holidays set a spiritual rhythm for the entire year. They each exercise the soul in different ways, offering times for pleasure and pain, celebration and sorrow. Holidays offer us a full-body emotional and spiritual workout. This cycle keeps us in shape for the ongoing dialogue with God. It helps us to be able to hear God's voice in the world. It shows us what to listen for. Third, holidays recap the story of our people. In particular, the biblical holidays recap the stages of the biblical journey and the teachings of the Bible itself. Historical holidays extend the journey and its stages. For example, the seder matches the book of Exodus, which is a retelling of the Exodus itself.

For the Christian reader of this book, Jewish holidays lend insight into the religious psyche of the Jewish people. They help to build a bridge of understanding and a common universe of discourse, especially when reviewing the Christian parallels that we have included in each chapter. As Judaism is the tradition out of which Christianity emerged, understanding the Jewish holidays will also give Christian readers insight into their own traditions. For example, understanding Passover will lead to a deeper sense of Easter, and examining Shavuot will illuminate Pentecost. We hope this book will help you in your own religious journey as you explore the Jewish holidays with us.

1

ROSH HASHANAH
EMBRACING THE NEW YEAR WITH AWE AND SELF-REFLECTION

> In the seventh month, on the first day of the month, you
> shall observe a sacred occasion; you shall not do any work.
> You shall observe it as a day when the horn is sounded.
> —LEVITICUS 29:1–2

Rosh Hashanah literally means the "head of the year." It is both a New Year's celebration and the beginning of a penitential period that culminates with Yom Kippur ten days later. In America, this ten-day period is known as the High Holidays or High Holy Days. In Hebrew, however, this period is called the *Yamim Noraim,* the "Days of Awe." Perhaps its Hebrew name is more fitting, because awe is at the core of the holiday. In this case, *awe* means something akin to deep fear. We experience fear on Rosh Hashanah because we are meant to come face to face with how little power we ultimately have over our lives. We feel deeply about how temporary our tenure is in this world, how fleeting our lives are. Simply put, people we know will die between one Rosh Hashanah and the next. We ourselves may die between one Rosh Hashanah and the next. On Rosh Hashanah we come before God to acknowledge our powerlessness in this world and to ask the One who gives life and who also takes life to grant us another year.

Once, about ten years ago I, Dan, served as the rabbi for Rosh Hashanah services for a congregation in Laramie,

1

Wyoming. During the High Holiday services I was conducting, it dawned on me that the Torah, the painstakingly hand-scribed copy of the Bible—the holiest object in Jewish tradition—was being housed in a gun rack.

A gun rack happens to be just the right size and shape to hold a Torah. At first I was mortified. Never having hunted even once in my life, never having shot a gun even once in my life, a gun rack seemed antithetical to the Torah, a symbol of peace. When I mentioned this to one of the congregants, he said quite calmly, "Rabbi, on Rosh Hashanah we are meant to feel the power of life and death—a gun rack will get us in that mind-set a heck of a lot quicker than any ordinary Torah ark."

I had to agree about that.

THE BASICS: ROSH HASHANAH AND THE PROMISE OF A NEW YEAR

As with many Jewish holidays, synagogue services and festive foods are the basic ways this holiday is marked. On Rosh Hashanah, services are held on the evening when the holiday begins and are followed by services the next two mornings (except in some Reform and Reconstructionist synagogues, where services may be held on only one morning).

Families from liberal congregations have meals together before services on the night of Rosh Hashanah; those who belong to more traditional congregations have them afterward. As for lunch the following day, families from both liberal and traditional congregations have this meal after services. Many families invite relatives and friends to share festive meals at this time.

On the one hand, Rosh Hashanah is a celebratory day. It marks the beginning of a new year, according to the Jewish religious calendar, somewhat akin to January 1 on the secular calendar; there is that feeling of joy that comes from flipping the calendar to a new year. But the Jewish religious calendar is different in that it marks time according to a complicated formula that was established millennia ago with regard to the marking of the rule of God as Sovereign Ruler, in much the same way that monarchies count years based on the rule of a particular king. The secular calendar, which Christians also use as their religious calendar, begins with the death of Jesus Christ. So the year 2006 on the secular calendar is the Hebrew year 5766. Most Jews do not take this calculation literally as a precise date, but we continue to employ this method for the sake of tradition.

Yet even as Rosh Hashanah is celebratory, its more significant aspect is not festive at all. Rather, it is reflective, for Rosh Hashanah marks the beginning of a ten-day penitential period that culminates on Yom Kippur. During this period we look back over the course of the past year to see whom we have hurt and to rectify those wrongs we have done. We are asked during this period to try to come back to living the life that we should be living. And we are asked to come back to God. The word for "coming back" or "returning" in Hebrew is *teshuvah,* and it is the central theme of the ten-day period of the High Holidays.

Thus, there are two profound ideas at the heart of Rosh Hashanah. The first is that we humble ourselves before God, who has the power to decree life and death. The second is that we are meant to turn away from things that are destructive and harmful and turn back toward God. Rabbi Arthur Green, a contemporary Jewish theologian, quotes a nineteenth-century rabbi named Yehuda Leib Alter of Ger to illuminate the two aspects of Rosh Hashanah. Rabbi Alter of Ger said that the human heart is the tablet on which God writes. Each of us has the word *life* engraved in our hearts by God's own hands. Over the course of a year, that engraving comes to be covered with grit. Our sins, our neglect of prayer and study, the very pace at which we live, all conspire to blot out the word *life* that still lies written deep within our hearts. On Rosh Hashanah we come before God, having cleansed ourselves as best we can, to ask God to write that word *life* again on our hearts.[1]

The Books of Life and Death

One of the central images during the High Holiday period is God as the author of two books: the book of life and the book of death. Those who have acted righteously in the previous year have their names written in the book of life and will live another year; those who have acted sinfully have their names inscribed in the book of death. The Talmud says that those who are completely righteous are entered into the book of life before Rosh Hashanah and those who are entirely sinners are entered into the book of death. Most of us, the Talmud says, are *beynonim* (a Hebrew word meaning "in between all righteous and all sinful") and are not written into either book before Rosh Hashanah begins. Our judgment is suspended until Yom Kippur; it is then that it will be decreed by God. The period between Rosh Hashanah and Yom Kippur is our time to encourage God through our actions to write our name into the book of life for the coming year. We have three ways to do this: prayer, repentance, and *tzedakah* (righteous acts of charity).

This imagery forms the heart of the essential prayer of the High Holidays, called the *Unetaneh Tokef* (literally, "Let us proclaim"). Following is the prayer in its entirety. Note the imagery of God as the author of life and death:

> Let us proclaim the sacred power of this day; it is awesome and full of dread.
>
> For on this day Your dominion is exalted, Your throne established in steadfast love; there in truth You reign.

In truth You are Arbiter, Counsel, and Witness.
You write and You seal, You record and recount.
You remember deeds long forgotten.

You open the book of our days, and what is written there
proclaims itself, for it bears the signature of every human
being.
The great shofar [ram's horn] is sounded, a still small voice
is heard; the angels, gripped by fear and trembling,
declare in awe: This is the Day of Judgment! For even
the hosts of heaven are judged as all who dwell on earth
stand arrayed before You.

As the shepherd seeks out the flock, and makes the sheep
pass under the staff, so do You muster and number and
consider every soul, setting the bounds of every creature's
life, and decreeing its destiny.

On Rosh Hashanah it is written and on Yom Kippur it is
sealed:
How many shall pass on and how many shall come to be;
Who shall live and who shall die;
Who shall see ripe old age and who shall not;
Who shall perish by fire and who by water;
Who by sword and who by wild beast;
Who by hunger and who by thirst;
Who by earthquake and who by plague;
Who by strangling and who by stoning;
Who shall be secure and who shall be driven;
Who shall be tranquil and who shall be troubled;
Who shall be poor and who shall be rich;
Who shall be humbled and who exalted.

But repentance, prayer, and charity temper judgment's
severe decree.

This is Your glory, You are slow to anger, ready to forgive,
Adonai [God], it is not the death of sinners You seek but
that they should turn from their ways and live.

Until the last day You wait for them, welcoming them as
soon as they turn to You.

You have created us and know what we are. We are but
flesh and blood.

The human origin is dust and dust is our end.

Each of us is a shattered urn, grass that must wither, a
flower that will fade, a shadow moving on, a cloud
passing by, a particle of dust floating on the wind, a
dream soon forgotten.

But You are the Sovereign Ruler, the everlasting God.

There are a number of striking elements in this prayer.
Perhaps the foremost aspect of the prayer is the graphic account-
ing of our impending death, if we do not repent. The gory detail
is certainly meant to instill a sense of fear, but we should not read
a statement of universal Jewish theology into this prayer. From
the book of Job onward, Jewish thinkers have struggled with,
and often rejected, the simple reward-and-punishment calculus
that this prayer implies. (See Dr. Neil Gillman's *The Jewish
Approach to God: A Brief Introduction for Christians* [Woodstock,
Vt.: Jewish Lights Publishing] for discussion on this question.)
Nonetheless, the visceral power of *Unetaneh Tokef,* the overwhelming feeling of dread it evokes, regardless of theology, is
what gives the prayer a central place in the High Holiday liturgy.
Of course, some of us will die and some of us will live in the
year to come. Some of us may die tragically, but we do not know
who among us will die in such a way. Thus, all we can do in the
face of this reality is to be humble, kind, and repentant.

Historical Background: The Origin and Development of Rosh Hashanah

There is surprisingly little mention of Rosh Hashanah in the Bible itself. When it is first mentioned in Leviticus, it does not even call the day by the name *Rosh Hashanah,* nor does it mention it as a festival of the new year, or as the beginning of a penitential period. The Bible, in fact, says that the holiday we now call Rosh Hashanah was the first day of the seventh month and was the start of the agricultural year—not the calendar year. The Bible says that on this day work will not be done, and it will be a day of praise marked by the sounding of the horn.

Some of the ideas and customs that we now identify as part of Rosh Hashanah had evolved by the period of the Mishnah in the first centuries of the common era. The Mishnah is part of the oral law traditionally believed to have been given at Mount Sinai alongside the Torah and eventually written down and codified in 200 CE. The blowing of the shofar, or ram's horn, as a central ritual emerges in the context of numerous discussions, such as in the various sounds the shofar can make and the various types of shofars that can be used. The Mishnah includes a discussion of whether the shofar itself can be straight or should be bent. The Rabbis of the Mishnah conclude that the shofar should be bent to reflect our humility as "bent" before God, rather than straight, which might suggest a haughtiness before God.

The Mishnah also notes that we are judged on Rosh Hashanah. But the full explication of this idea does not come until four hundred years later in the Talmud, which is the entire text of the oral law, including the Mishnah. The Talmud specifies that Rosh Hashanah is the beginning of a ten-day reflective period. This holds true today.

Rosh Hashanah Customs and Observances

Rosh Hashanah is distinguished by a variety of rituals that reflect its celebration as the Jewish New Year. Each ritual observance contributes a significant and specific meaning to the holiday, attempting to take an abstract idea and make it more concrete. By developing an understanding of these various rituals, personal observance can be enriched and spiritual experience, elevated.

Preparing for Rosh Hashanah

As a sign of the importance of the High Holidays, Jewish tradition requires us to prepare for them well ahead of time. We are not meant to just show up at Rosh Hashanah services and think of ourselves as ready for the holiday. As a colleague of ours used to remark, it is like showing up for the day of the big race without having trained beforehand. The work of *teshuvah* (repentance) takes inspiration and effort. According to Jewish tradition, the spiritual preparation for Rosh Hashanah begins exactly one month before the High Holidays.

Two rituals mark the preparation for Rosh Hashanah. The first is the sounding of the shofar every day of the month after morning prayer services, except on Shabbat. The shofar is a ram's horn associated with the holiday, as described below. The other ritual that begins the month prior to Rosh Hashanah is the daily recitation of Psalm 27. This psalm is recited primarily because of its reference to salvation: "Adonai [God] is my light and my salvation. Whom shall I fear? Adonai is the strength of my life. Of whom shall I be afraid?" The Midrash, or commentary of parables on the Scriptures, on the psalm says that the light of Adonai refers specifically to Rosh Hashanah, while the salvation of Adonai is a reference to Yom Kippur.[2]

Both of these rituals are meant to encourage us to reflect on the meaningful themes of Rosh Hashanah. The sound of the shofar is taken to be a clarion call, a wake-up to those who hear it to turn their hearts and souls toward repentance. In Psalm 27, the psalmist reflects our fear and anxiety about our place in the world: "Do not hide Your face from me; do not put Your servant away in anger; You have been my help; do not abandon me, nor forsake me, O God of my salvation." But despite the anxiety that God will abandon us, we also declare our hope: "Wait for Adonai; be of good courage, and God will strengthen your heart; wait for Adonai."

Selichot (Penitential Prayers)

The preparation for Rosh Hashanah reaches its climax with *Selichot*. *Selichot* refers to a collection of penitential prayers. Jews of Eastern European heritage (Ashkenazic Jews) hold a special *Selichot* service in the early morning on the days just before Rosh Hashanah, while Jews from Spanish and North African descent (Sephardic Jews) read these prayers every morning during the month before Rosh Hashanah. An American custom has developed to hold *Selichot* services at midnight, generally on the Saturday night directly preceding Rosh Hashanah. Praying at midnight is part of the Jewish mystical tradition. Jewish mystics believe that a person's prayers are more likely to be answered by God if prayed at midnight.

Shofar

The shofar, an animal horn blown during services on the holiday, is the most recognizable symbol of Rosh Hashanah. The shofar is typically made from a ram's horn, but the horn of any kosher animal can be used, except for a cow or an ox.

9

Although it is an important symbol of the holiday, there is no one meaning as to why we sound the shofar. The medieval Jewish scholar Saadiah Gaon offers ten different meanings for the sounding of the shofar. We offer here a few of his reasons:

> The shofar's blasts are like the trumpets that announce the coronation of a king. By sounding the shofar we are acknowledging God's dominion over the world.
>
> The sound of the shofar stirs us to do *teshuvah,* to figure out where we have gone astray and return to God.
>
> The sound of the shofar reminds us of Mount Sinai, where God gave the Torah, because the Torah records that a shofar was sounded at the moment of revelation.

The shofar reminds us of the story of Abraham's binding of Isaac (Genesis 22). Abraham ultimately sacrifices a ram in place of his son, so the shofar, which is typically a ram's horn, recalls this episode in the life of Abraham and Isaac. This story, known in Hebrew as the *Akedah* (literally, "the Binding"), is read as part of the public Torah reading on the second day of Rosh Hashanah. The story of Abraham's willingness to sacrifice his son is a troubling story, and Jewish commentators have long disagreed about the meaning of the story and why it is read on Rosh Hashanah. Saadiah Gaon understands that the story exemplifies the faith in God to which we all should aspire.

Another well-known explanation for the sounding of the shofar comes from the Hasidic tradition. The Hasidic rabbis often communicated their ideas through stories, and the following story tells of the rabbi and a broken heart.

> Once, the founder of Hasidism, the Baal Shem Tov, instructed a shofar blower on the mystical meanings of the shofar blasts. On Rosh Hashanah, as he was blowing the

shofar, he was meant to think of these mystical intentions. But on Rosh Hashanah the blower forgot everything he had learned from the rabbi and so he broke down in tears. The Baal Shem Tov told him that the mystical meanings were like keys to the many doors of Heaven. But if the keys are all lost, the doors can be broken open by an axe. And so the heartbroken burst of tears can break down all the barriers between ourselves and God. The shofar's untuned wail, its sobbing, is that burst of human tears.[3]

Apples and Honey

It is customary to eat apples and honey after Rosh Hashanah services at the synagogue and at home. The apples and honey symbolize the hope for a sweet new year.

Tashlikh

On the afternoon of the first day of Rosh Hashanah (or the second day, if the first day falls on Shabbat), a unique ceremony is held. Worshipers gather near the closest body of water to their synagogue to perform the *tashlikh* ritual. The ritual begins by taking bread crumbs and putting them in your pockets. After certain verses of the Bible are recited, you empty your pockets into the water. The bread crumbs symbolize your sins of the past year, and the sprinkling of them in water is a symbol of your desire to avoid repeating these sins in the coming year. The origins of the ceremony are unclear. As with almost all Jewish rituals, there is a variety of customs among Jews as to how to perform this ritual. The Jews of Kurdistan, for example, went to the river and instead of tossing bread crumbs, they jumped fully clothed into the river.

CHRISTIAN PARALLELS TO ROSH HASHANAH

The "New Year" for the Western Christian calendar is the holiday season of Advent. Like Rosh Hashanah, Advent marks the beginning of a holiday cycle. It comes four weeks before Christmas and begins the preparation for celebrating the birth of Jesus. Just as Rosh Hashanah has two components—the joy implicit in anticipating a new year and soulful self-reflection before Yom Kippur—Advent historically had two components. Initially, Advent was observed by fasting and penitence.

Advent anticipates the Nativity, the birth of Jesus. In Christian theology, Jesus's birth is intertwined with his crucifixion. Thus, Advent is connected to Lent, the forty-day period prior to Easter. And just as Lent marks a period of penitence, so Advent was initially observed in the same way. Since Jesus died for the sins of the people, Christians were required to reflect on their lives and take steps toward purifying themselves from sin. The Eastern Orthodox Church still infuses Advent with a sense of penitence.

For the Western church, however, Advent is primarily now a holiday of hope and anticipation. Similar to the joyful aspects of Rosh Hashanah, it looks toward a new beginning. The holidays are, of course, different in their understanding of a new beginning. The hope of Advent is the belief that Jesus will come again and the world will be transformed as a result. In Rosh Hashanah, the hope is more inwardly focused—the hope that all of us will be granted another year of life so that we can continue to do the work of God in the world.

2

Yom Kippur
Atoning for Sins and Renewing Life

It shall be a Sabbath of complete rest for you, and you shall practice self-denial; it is a law for all time.

—Leviticus 16:29

Yom Kippur literally means "Day of Atonement." It marks the end of a ten-day penitential period that begins with Rosh Hashanah and is the holiest day of the Jewish year. Abraham Joshua Heschel, one of the most significant Jewish theologians of the twentieth century, called Yom Kippur "Judaism's great cathedral." Not a physical cathedral of stones and stained-glass windows, but a cathedral built of a day.[1] For thousands of years, Jews have understood that on this day, more than any other, it was possible to meet God.

One of the more famous stories about Yom Kippur comes from the life of a renowned Jewish philosopher. In 1913 in Germany, Franz Rosenzweig left a note for his mother that he was going to convert to Christianity. This was not an unusual step in Germany at the time. A fellow philosopher and friend had converted to Christianity and had convinced Rosenzweig to follow suit. As a last step before embracing the church, Rosenzweig went to Yom Kippur service in Berlin. But something happened at that Yom Kippur service. Afterward, he decided not to convert. He never wrote or spoke about exactly what happened to him at the prayer service that caused him to change his mind, but we can guess what he experienced. Rosenzweig writes, "Man is utterly alone on the day of his death, and in the prayers of this day [Yom Kippur] he is utterly alone as well ... as if he were dead in the midst of life.... And [then] God lifts up His countenance to this plead-ing of men."[2]

Rosenzweig's phrase about being "dead in the midst of life," although seemingly morbid, captures the essence of the day. One of the traditional customs of the holiday is to wear a burial shroud, called a *kittel,* during prayer on Yom Kippur. The wearing of a burial shroud symbolizes that on Yom Kippur we suffer a form of death in life. We also experience redemption from that death in life. God redeems those who have come back through *teshuvah,* repentance. On this day the Jewish soul comes closest to God, because on this day we experience the cycle of death and rebirth.

The Basics: Yom Kippur and Repentance

At the heart of Yom Kippur is *teshuvah*—repentance. Yom Kippur beseeches us to seek forgiveness from other people, and then from God, for all the wrongs we have committed in the previous year. Judaism distinguishes between wrongs commit-ted against God and wrongs committed against other people. The Rabbis in the Mishnah put it this way: "Yom Kippur effects atonement for transgressions that are between God and humans; but for transgressions between humans, Yom Kippur effects atonement only if one has appeased one's fellow" (*Mishnah Yoma* 8:9). This idea is crucial to observing Yom Kippur. On Yom Kippur, if we are sincere in repenting toward God, atonement is granted for those sins related to God (for example, not praying, not observing ritual commandments). But regarding people whom we have wronged, Judaism calls on us to approach those people and seek forgiveness directly from them. This constitutes an important difference between Judaism and Roman Catholicism. According to Catholic theology, absolution is given through the confessional, in the sacrament of reconciliation. In Judaism, there is no confessional for wrongs committed against others. Absolution can only be given by the person who has been wronged. Jewish tradition holds that if the person who has been hurt refuses to forgive, the one seeking forgiveness has to return three times to ask for forgiveness. The obligation to make *teshuvah*, repentance, is just as strong in Judaism as is the obligation to return to God. This is why it is customary for some Jews to call friends and family in the days leading up to Yom Kippur and ask forgiveness for any wrongs committed during the previous year, so they can enter Yom Kippur free to focus on repentance toward God.

The great medieval Jewish philosopher Moses Maimonides outlined three steps in repentance toward others. The first step is to acknowledge the wrong committed and make amends for any damage caused. The second step is to commit to not repeating the mistake again. The third step is, when confronted with the same set of circumstances, not to make the same mistake again. Maimonides writes it this way, "What is complete repentance? Perfect repentance is when an opportunity presents itself to the offender for repeating the offense and he refrains from committing it because of his repentance, and not out of fear or physical inability."[3]

A famous rabbinic parable tells us that God created *teshuvah*, repentance, before God created the world. In other words, God knew even before creating the world that people would need an opportunity to start over again. There is such pathos and truthful understanding of the human condition in this parable. At its core, repentance provides the Jewish soul with an opportunity to acknowledge mistakes, while having the hope of beginning again.

HISTORICAL BACKGROUND: THE ORIGIN AND DEVELOPMENT OF YOM KIPPUR

The Bible establishes the parameters for most holiday observances. However, since Judaism is a Rabbinic religion, that is, the Bible as seen through the lenses of the Rabbis, it is important to consider the evolution of a holiday and its practices over time.

In the Bible

Yom Kippur is mentioned three times in the Bible. In two places, Leviticus 23:27 and Numbers 29:7, it is included in a list of all the other holidays. In Leviticus 16:29 it says that each Israelite should "observe a day of sacred occasion when you shall practice self-denial. You shall do no work." Practicing self-denial primarily means fasting. On Yom Kippur, we fast from the sundown that marks the beginning of the holiday to the next evening. The Torah then continues by directing each person to bring sacrificial offerings as atonement. The Torah is characteristically quite sparse in its explanation of the reason to observe this holiday. There is nothing in the Torah about this day as the most important day of the year, or about personal repentance; these ideas developed later. What the Torah does offer is a lengthy description of the Temple ritual that the priest, the religious leader of the community responsible for the ancient Temple and its sacrificial cult, performed on Yom Kippur when the Temple was standing (950–586 BCE and 541 BCE–70 CE).

In Leviticus 16, the Torah outlines the priestly obligation to purify the Temple. The high priest donned specially made white linen vestments and cleansed himself with water before beginning the purification ritual. The text then describes the unusual ritual for Yom Kippur. The high priest took two male goats and placed them near the altar to God. One goat was randomly chosen as a sacrifice for God, while the other goat was chosen as a sacrifice for Azazel. Who or what was Azazel? Biblical critics and commentators have asked the same question. The next part of the ritual may provide some clue to this mystery.

After the sacrifice of the goat was made for God, the goat for Azazel was brought forward: "Aaron [the high priest] shall lay both his hands upon the head of the live goat and confess over it all of the iniquities and transgressions of the Israelites, whatever their sins, putting them on the head of the goat; and it shall be sent off to the wilderness" (Leviticus 16:21). A well-known sixteenth-century English translation of the Bible refers to the goat that was carrying away the sins of Israel into the wilderness as the *scapegoat*. This is the first time in the English language that this phrase is used. The scapegoat was thus the goat for Azazel, sent to wander into the wilderness. Generally, two possibilities are offered as explanations of Azazel. Either Azazel is some sort of demon that is meant to be appeased on Yom Kippur by the goat, or Azazel represents a desire on our part to remove ourselves from the inclination to do evil and to have that inclination wander off into the wilderness.

Other sacrifices conducted by the high priest on Yom Kippur were also unusual. He first sacrificed a bull to make atonement for himself and his household. Then he sacrificed a male goat to God to make atonement for the people. Next he purified the sanctuary itself. This rite was the only one in which Aaron entered the "Holy of Holies" with sacrificial blood. The Holy of Holies was considered the place where God's presence resided in the Temple. The priest entered this sanctuary with trepidation, afraid that being in such close proximity to God might kill him. The Torah makes it clear that a person cannot see God's face and live. Although modern Jews no longer practice sacrifice, or have priests, there is still the sense that on Yom Kippur we come into the Holy of Holies. On this day, we come as close as possible to God. And just as the high priest feared for his life when entering the Holy of Holies on this day, modern Jews also say that they enter Yom Kippur with fear and trembling in the presence of God's power.

One of the most powerful understandings of Yom Kippur comes from the prophet Isaiah, who addresses the obligations of Jews on fast days (Isaiah 58). It is customary in synagogues to read this chapter on Yom Kippur. In this chapter, Isaiah excoriates the Israelites for their hypocrisy:

> Behold, in the day of your fast you pursue your business, and exact all your payments. Behold, you fast for strife and debate, and to smite with the fist of wickedness. You fast not this day to make your voice to be heard on high. Is such the fast that I have chosen? A day for humans to afflict the soul? Is it to bow down one's head like a bulrush, and to spread sackcloth and ashes under oneself? Will you call this a fast, and an acceptable day to Adonai? Is not this rather the fast that I have chosen—to loosen the chains of the wickedness, to undo the bands of the yoke, and to let the oppressed go free, and to break every yoke? Is it not to share your bread with the hungry and bring the poor that are cast out into your house? When you see the naked, do you not cover him, and do you not hide yourself from your own flesh? Then shall your light break forth like the morning and your healing shall spring forth speedily, and righteousness shall go before you, the glory of Adonai shall be your rear guard. Then shall you

call and Adonai will answer; you shall cry out and God will say, "Here I am." (Isaiah 58:3–9)

Isaiah's eloquence is a powerful message on the meaning of Yom Kippur. Isaiah understands that ascetic practices like fasting often lead us into a type of narcissism. We become intoxicated with the sense that we are exceptionally holy for sacrificing something like food for a day. The fasting of Yom Kippur, however, is not performed so that we can feel pure; rather, the fasting should remind us of those who are in need of food and shelter. The call of Yom Kippur is not only to be humble, but to have that humility shine a light on all those in need of help.

In the Mishnah

The Mishnah, the oral tradition later incorporated in the Talmud, describes in detail the Temple service that took place on Yom Kippur. The high priest began preparing for Yom Kippur a week in advance. He presided over all the sacrifices that week. On the evening before Yom Kippur, he was attended to by other priests. Those who attended to his needs made sure that the high priest would not fall asleep; he remained awake all night long so that nothing could happen during his sleep that would possibly render him ritually impure. On the day of Yom Kippur, he entered the Holy of Holies. There the high priest uttered the secret name of God; upon hearing him say God's name, all those who were gathered outside the Holy of Holies fell prostrate on the ground and exclaimed, "Praised is the name of God forever" (*Mishnah Yoma* 6:2) (words that are now part of the *Shema*—Judaism's central creedal prayer statement).

The idea that God had a secret name is worth noting. God's Hebrew name has four letters in it: *yud-heh-vav-heh* (יהוה).

The name for God is connected with the verb "to be." Many commentators have suggested that this connection says something about the essence of God. God is being itself, or, as the Torah has God saying to Moses when Moses asks for God's name at the burning bush, "Tell them my name is 'I will be who I will be'" (Exodus 3:14). The secret of God's name is contained in its pronunciation rather than in its letters. Since those letters are Hebrew consonants and no vowels are given in the Bible, it is as if God's name were written as "Gd"—we have to figure out whether to have an "ah" or an "eh" or an "oo" sound in the middle of the consonants. According to Jewish tradition, the correct pronunciation was known only by the high priest; apparently this information was lost with the destruction of the Temple in 70 CE.

Since we do not know how to pronounce God's name, Jewish tradition maintains that we should scrupulously avoid even trying to pronounce it. So when *yud-heh-vav-heh* is written in the prayer book, Jews insert the Hebrew word for master, *Adonai,* in its place, although this word is spelled entirely differently. When the four letters are used, the vowels for *Adonai* are placed under it as a reminder of how it should be pronounced. Some Christian translations of the Bible mistakenly read this as either "Yahweh" or "Jehovah." Contrary to popular belief, these two names are not used by Jews.

Jewish tradition understands that names have power. Since Adam was charged with naming the animals in the garden, he was then given dominion over them. As a result, there are some who believe that it is better that we do not know the correct way of pronouncing God's name. If we knew how to do so, it might somehow give us power over God, a power that would be dangerous for us to control. This is all part of the reason why the Yom Kippur rite in the Temple was so central to Judaism. Only at one time of the year could a human being fully encounter God, speaking God's name, standing in the place where heaven and earth touched.

In the Talmud

If you were to walk into a synagogue on Yom Kippur, you might be surprised to see the extent of self-affliction taking place on such a solemn day. It is a custom on Yom Kippur to gently beat one's chest over the heart with one hand as a sign of contrition during the Yom Kippur confessionals. The confessional prayers were developed after the destruction of the Temple, as part of the process of atonement.

The Rabbis of the Talmud developed a liturgy of confession for Yom Kippur. A version of the confessional prayer recited at Yom Kippur appears below:

> Now may it be your will, Adonai, God of all generations,
>   to forgive all of our sins, to pardon all our wrongdoings,
>   and to blot out all our transgressions.
> For the sin we have committed against You under duress
>   or by choice,
> For the sin we have committed against You openly or
>   secretly,
> For the sin we have committed against You in our
>   thoughts,
> For the sin we have committed against You with our words,
> For the sin we have committed against You by the abuse of
>   power,
> For all these, God of mercy, forgive us, pardon us, grant us
>   atonement.
> For the sin we have committed against You by hardening
>   our hearts,

> For the sin we have committed against You by profaning
> Your name,
> For the sin we have committed against You by disrespect to
> our parents and teachers,
> For the sin we have committed against You by speaking
> slander,
> For the sin we have committed against You by dishonesty
> in our work,
> For the sin we have committed against You by hurting
> others in any way,
> For all these, God of mercy, forgive us, pardon us, grant us
> atonement.

Note that the confession of sins is expressed in the plural form. All the worshipers in the community recount their sins together. This may seem at odds with the idea of Yom Kippur as a time for individual atonement. There are many explanations for this construction of liturgy. Some liturgists have suggested that each of us is responsible for all the others, so their sins reflect on all of us. Some have suggested that a communal recitation of sins reminds us that our sins are often a reflection of the community's own weaknesses. Another reason offered for the public recitation of sins is that those in prayer will be motivated to think about ways in which they went astray without realizing it.

After the Temple was destroyed, there was no Holy of Holies for the high priest to enter. So Yom Kippur became focused primarily on *teshuvah,* repentance. As described above, repenting for wrongs done to others and to God shapes the core of the day. The Mishnah specifies the necessity to repent and adds that wrongdoing with the foreknowledge that one is going to repent is not acceptable: "If a person said: I will sin and repent and sin again and repent, that person will be given no chance to repent. [If that person said] I will sin and the day of Yom Kippur will make atonement for me, then Yom Kippur effects no atonement" (*Mishnah Yoma* 8:8).

The name of the confessional prayer noted above is *Al Cheyt,* translated here as "For the sin...." But a more nuanced understanding of the word for *sin* is instructive. The word *cheyt* (sin) is the same word used to describe the action of an arrow missing its mark. The idea is that when we sin, we miss the mark, the way an archer may miss the target. The process of redemption is the process of redirecting the archer's arrow toward the proper target. Sin does not stain the soul. If we can make proper atonement, then we have the ability to become renewed and be written in the book of life for another year. Depending on our actions during the previous year, God will write our names in one of two places; God will either record it in the book of life or the book of death—which determines if we will live or die in the upcoming year. The hope is, of course, to make proper atonement and live for another year (see chapter 1).

YOM KIPPUR CUSTOMS AND OBSERVANCES

While the Jewish religion is concerned with Jewish law since that is what primarily directs observances, there are many customs that shape holiday observances even more significantly than ritual that is prescribed by law. One generation's creativity often becomes community custom—and it then becomes more binding than law.

Fasting

As noted above, the Torah itself tells us to "afflict our souls" on Yom Kippur; this is interpreted to mean fasting, perhaps one of Judaism's most widely observed rituals. Even Jews who only go to synagogue once a year, for Yom Kippur, often fast on this day. The Mishnah describes other restrictions for Yom Kippur, which include refraining from sexual relations and not bathing (a self-indulgent luxury). In addition, leather-soled shoes are not worn because they are considered too comfortable. However, there is also a manifest sensitivity to the animal's life, whose hide was used to make the leather; that life is also considered sacred. The prohibition on wearing leather shoes prompts many Jews to go to synagogue in canvas sneakers on Yom Kippur.

Kol Nidre

Kol Nidre ("All Vows") is the prayer service on the evening of Yom Kippur, named for the prayer that introduces the evening service and serves as its leitmotif. (Since Jewish holidays start at sunset, this is the first service of the holiday.) This prayer has a controversial history. It asks God to forgive vows taken for the year ahead that may not be fulfilled. It may be construed as letting people "off the hook" ahead of time. If people begin the year by repenting for vows to be broken during the coming year, some may question the value of the vows in the first place.

Vows are considered sacred oaths in Jewish tradition, and they should never be taken lightly. The Bible says, "When you make any vow to Adonai your God, you must pay it without delay.... If you refrain from making a vow, that is no sin for you; but you must be careful to perform any promise you have made with your lips" (Deuteronomy 23:22). There is an entire tractate, or major section, of the Talmud that deals with oaths and under what circumstances we can declare an oath null and void. The nullification of an unfulfilled vow allows us to enter into a relationship with God. The Kol Nidre prayer arose out of the need for reconciliation between God and us over vows that were not kept.

The meaning of the prayer is not clear. The debate over its meaning is fueled by the existence of different versions of the prayer. In one version, the prayer refers to all vows made in the past year. The version of *Kol Nidre* used in most American synagogues refers to vows that will be made in the coming year. Either way, the prayer has been attacked at various times and even removed from the liturgy altogether by some rabbis who felt that it permits people to renege on their word. Some rabbis defend the prayer by saying that the vows referred to in the prayer are vows between the individual and God, rather than vows that reflect a relationship between two individuals. This defense is not meant to convey that it is acceptable to break a vow with God, but rather to highlight the purpose of the *Kol Nidre* prayer, which is to seek forgiveness and atonement from God, rather than from other people, should a vow be broken. The practical concern is that people might use *Kol Nidre* to get out of a business transaction. Because of its content, some Christians historically have used it as part of anti-Jewish propaganda to suggest that Jews were untrustworthy. In some instances in European history, Jews had to swear a "Jew's oath" because of the concerns of Christian authorities over the *Kol Nidre* prayer. Nevertheless, the prayer remains at the center of the most solemn service of the year.

Kol Nidre even has an unusual choreography. Torah scrolls are taken out of the holy ark (the closet in the front of the sanctuary reserved for Torah scrolls) as all those in the congregation rise. The people holding the scrolls stand on either side of the cantor (the person who chants the prayer). The cantor chants the prayer three times, customarily raising his or her voice each time it is sung. The mood in the synagogue during the chanting of *Kol Nidre* is somber. The melody is plaintive and haunting.

At the conclusion of the *Kol Nidre* chant, the cantor sings the well-known Jewish prayer called the *Shehecheyanu*: "Praised is God, Sovereign of the world, who has given us life, sustained us, and brought us to this moment." One famous contemporary rabbi, Joseph Soleveitchik, remarked that the most important moment of the year for him was the recitation of that blessing after *Kol Nidre,* because it proved to him he had survived another year.[4]

The *Kol Nidre* prayer is translated as follows:

[First, those holding Torah scrolls join with the cantor and say:] In the tribunal of heaven and the tribunal of earth, by the permission of God—the Holy Blessed One—and by the permission of this holy congregation, we hold it lawful to pray with the transgressors.

[The cantor chants three times:] All vows, obligations, oaths, and anathemas, pledges of all names which we may vow, or swear, or pledge, or whereby we may be bound, from this Day of Atonement until the next (whose happy coming we await), we do repent. May they be deemed absolved, forgiven, annulled, and void, and made of no effect; they shall not bind us nor have power over us. The vows shall not be reckoned vows; the obligations shall not be obligatory; nor the oaths be oaths.

[The congregation recites Numbers 15:26:] And it shall be forgiven all the congregation of Israelites and the stranger that sojourns among them, seeing all the people were in ignorance.

The Great Aleinu

The Great *Aleinu* refers to a specific prayer recited during the day of Yom Kippur. While the *Aleinu* prayer is recited at every Jewish prayer service (three times a day), the *Aleinu* prayer on Yom Kippur is called "great" because it is at that moment when the prayer leader lies fully prostrate in front of the Torah ark, an act that hearkens back to the high priest entering the Holy of Holies. Jews bow at other points during the service throughout the year, but just as the high priest entered the Holy of Holies only once during the year, Jews prostrate themselves only this one time during the year. It is an act of utter humility to lie down before God, an act that is consistent with the theme of humbleness that marks the entire day.

Kaparah

Kaparah (literally, "atonement") is an unusual Jewish custom. It is practiced today only by a small group of Orthodox Jews in the United States and throughout the world. Just before Yom Kippur, a person waves a live chicken around their head three times, while a prayer is said that transfers the sins of the person to the chicken. The chicken is then slaughtered, and its meat is given to the poor. Since the Middle Ages, some Jews have used money in place of a chicken. Like the chicken, the money is waved around the head three times while a prayer is recited, and then it is given away as charity. This custom is reminiscent of the goat that was sent off into the wilderness.

Kittel

The *kittel* is a burial shroud that is also worn on Yom Kippur. Unlike its use for burial when it clothes the dead body, on Yom Kippur it is worn over clothing. Made of soft white cloth, the *kittel* is traditionally used for both men and women for burial, but only men wear it for Yom Kippur. In egalitarian synagogues that have adopted this custom, both men and women may be seen wearing *kittels*. Although some people may view it as a morbid custom, the practice reflects the central theme of

Yom Kippur: We need to confront our own mortality and live every day of our lives as if it were our last, and we are born anew each new day.

CHRISTIAN PARALLELS TO YOM KIPPUR

There is no holiday on the Christian calendar that is a direct parallel to Yom Kippur, but Ash Wednesday is a day that reflects many of the same ideas and symbols as Yom Kippur. The placing of ashes on the forehead as a symbol of mortality—ashes to ashes, dust to dust (adapted from Genesis 3:19)—is similar to the custom of wearing a burial shroud on Yom Kippur. On both days, the worshiper's confrontation with mortality may lead to contrition and atonement.

Ash Wednesday also begins a forty-day period of abstinence. Traditionally, Roman Catholics give up meat on Fridays and have only one full meatless meal a day during Ash Wednesday and Good Friday of the Lenten period. This austerity is similar to the fasting of Yom Kippur, where abstention from food is meant to focus our thoughts on repentance. In the Episcopal tradition, Isaiah 58 is sometimes read as part of the Ash Wednesday liturgy. As discussed above, Isaiah 58 is one of the central liturgical pieces of the Yom Kippur service. It warns the worshiper that fasting should be done to inspire those who fast to help those less fortunate, not simply to feel pious in their asceticism.

The Episcopal Book of Common Prayer includes the following prayer as part of the Ash Wednesday liturgy; the correspondence with the Yom Kippur confessional is striking:

> Most holy and merciful Father:
> We confess to You and to one another,
> and to the whole communion of saints

in heaven and on earth,

that we have sinned by our own fault

in thought, word, and deed;

by what we have done, and by what we have left undone.

In the Roman Catholic Church, this prayer (and its continuation) is called the *Confiteor* ("I confess") and is recited by the priest and congregation at every mass.

In comparing the themes expressed in this brief prayer with those elucidated in this chapter, the overlap is obvious. In both there is a confession of sins to others as well as to God; the clear recognition of wrongdoing; and an acknowledgment that some of our sins are sins of omission—what we could have done, but did not do—as well as sins of commission. Both Jewish and Christian traditions value penitence and recognize that there is a human need to set aside a period of time on the religious calendar to focus on shortcomings and to ask the Holy One to forgive us for instances where we have gone astray.

3

SUKKOT

BUILDING HUTS AND ENJOYING THE HARVEST

> You should rejoice in your festival [Sukkot] with your son
> and your daughter.... You shall hold the festival for God
> seven days in the place that God will choose. For God will
> bless all your crops and all your undertakings, and you
> shall have nothing but joy.
>
> —DEUTERONOMY 16:14–15

The police were at the door. It was the first night of Sukkot, and we were eating dinner in our backyard in the *sukkah*, a small shelter built for the holiday. Normally I, Dan, am a law-abiding citizen, so I was surprised to hear an emphatic knocking at my door, even after seeing the police car's flashing lights in my driveway. The officers said that they had gotten a report of loud noises and an "unidentifiable structure" in the back-yard of my home. My neighbor must have called them, concerned about the late-night singing (in words she didn't understand) and the makeshift hut in my backyard. We told the police that the "unidentifiable structure" was a *sukkah*, a small lean-to that is built to celebrate the holiday of Sukkot. We also told the police officers that Sukkot is a festival that requires Jews to build small huts (*sukkot,* plural of *sukkah*) in their backyards to recall the huts the Israelites built for shelter during the forty years of wandering in the wilderness. By the time my wife and I were done with our explanation, the police were clearly bewildered. They had thought they were on a routine nuisance complaint, and here they were face to face with excited Jews going on about the wanderings in the wilderness. "Well, then, okay, I guess ...," one officer mumbled as he shuffled out the door.

Sukkot is an eight-day festival that occurs five days after Yom Kippur. There are two components to the holiday. One aspect of the holiday is a joyful celebration of the fall harvest, practiced since ancient times. The other feature of Sukkot is the building of temporary booths *(sukkot)* like the ones that sheltered the Israelites during their wanderings in the Sinai desert. The fragility of the booths reminds us that the real solidity in our lives is God's presence and not material things: houses, cars, clothes, and the like. Just prior to the holiday, Jews build these *sukkot* in their backyards, and they eat and even sleep in them. Sukkot is the most tactile of all the Jewish holiday periods. Although mysterious to the uninitiated, Sukkot also encompasses other special days (Hoshanah Rabbah and Shemini Atzeret, in particular, explained later in this chapter) and concludes with another festival, Simchat Torah, covered in chapter 4.

THE BASICS: SUKKOT AND THE CELEBRATION OF NATURE

The holiday of Sukkot, sometimes referred to as *Hechag* ("the Festival") in the Bible (Leviticus 23:39–40), celebrates both history and nature. After the Israelites were redeemed from Egypt, they wandered through the Sinai desert without shelter. The Bible tells us that they lived in booths for forty years under God's protection, but we do not know exactly what the booths looked like. Today Jews approximate what they might have looked like by building small wooden huts. Many Jews build these booths in their backyards or on their porches or decks. Almost all synagogues build *sukkot* for communal use and for use by those who cannot build their own.

Jewish tradition directs members of the Jewish community to begin the process of building the *sukkah* in the moments after Yom Kippur ends. Although most Jews do not start building a wooden hut immediately after fasting for over twenty-four hours, some Jews do symbolically erect one pole for the *sukkah* as a sign of their desire to move immediately from one holiday to the next.

Jewish law says that the *sukkah* must have more than two walls and must be big enough for someone to take meals inside it. Perhaps the most important rule regarding the construction of a *sukkah* is that it must be a temporary structure. This is its main message: As God protected the Israelites on their precarious journey through the wilderness, so God will protect us on our precarious journey through this world.

The ceiling of the *sukkah* must be made of organic material that is already detached from the ground when it is found, such as tree branches or palm fronds. We are not permitted to destroy anything living to put on top of the *sukkah*. This material is called *sechach*. The important rule of *sechach* is that we cannot put so much on the top of the *sukkah* that we can no longer see the stars. The stars are a symbol of God's presence.

Sukkot is also called *z'man simchateinu,* "the time of our joy." Because the holiday occurs so soon after Yom Kippur, where we have come face to face with our mortality (see chapter 2), the holiday of Sukkot is something of a relief. We exhale the solemnity of Yom Kippur and embrace a holiday where we bring palms and lemonlike citrons (see *lulav* and *etrog* below) to the synagogue.

Historical Background: The Origin and Background of Sukkot

Sukkot begins on the twenty-second of the month of Tishrei, corresponding to a date in September or October that varies from year to year. It resembles Passover in that both holidays begin a season and celebrate a harvest. Because Sukkot is associated with the fall holiday season and represents its conclusion, it is extremely important in the religious calendar. At Sukkot we make a "clean start" for a new year.

When the Israelites reached the Land of Israel, they became farmers. During the fall harvest, they built booths that they used to protect them from the sun during the harvest. As a result, Sukkot became a holiday that celebrates both the harvest and the forty years of wandering. The *sukkah* became a symbol of God's protection, and the holiday became a time for feasting and thanksgiving. In Jewish liturgy, the imagery of a *sukkah* as God's protection remains significant. At every evening prayer service, or at bedtime, we ask God to spread a *sukkat shalom,* a "shelter of peace," over Israel. Because of the harvest nature of the holiday, Sukkot was originally referred to as *Chag Ha-asif* ("the Gathering Festival").

The eighth day of Sukkot is singled out as Shemini Atzeret ("Eighth Day of Assembly"). It is a more somber time than the rest of the festival, and its most salient element is a prayer for rain. The other elements continue on this day as well: candlelighting, festive food and clothing, and blessings over wine and bread.

Sukkot Customs and Observances

Sukkot is probably the most colorful and most public of the Jewish holidays. There are numerous customs that take place during the holiday that make it special, especially coming so soon after the intensive introspective period of the High Holidays. The theme of the fall harvest informs all of these customs.

The Sukkah

The distinctive feature of Sukkot is the *sukkah,* built just for the holiday, in which meals are eaten. It is a custom to invite friends and family over for these festive meals. *Sukkot* are often decorated with symbols of nature, such as gourds. The commandment is to dwell in the *sukkah,* so some people sleep in them as well. Jewish law does not demand extreme measures in this regard, so if it is cold or raining outside, we need not sack out under the stars.

    Sukkot themselves are usually made out of wood with simple two-by-fours attached together to create the outline of walls. Some people use blankets or thin wooden sheets to make "walls" for the *sukkah.* In Jerusalem, a close inspection of the apartment buildings reveals that terraces are generally not built one directly on top of the other, as might be the case in cities like New York. This is to allow each apartment to build a *sukkah* during the holiday with a direct view of the stars above. The building of the *sukkah* is often like an old-fashioned barn raising. Friends may come over and, in an hour or two, a sturdy *sukkah* can be put up by three or four people. Some synagogues sponsor a *sukkah*-building event, in which teams of builders go from home to home, building a *sukkah* for those who are unable to build one themselves. Because we live in a wondrous technological age, premade *sukkot* can be ordered online. It comes in a box, and we need only put in a few screws to build it.

The Four Species

The Bible designates four plants required for the observance of the holiday. According to Leviticus, "On the first day you shall take the fruit of goodly trees, branches of palm trees, boughs of leafy trees, and willows of the brook, and you shall rejoice before God seven days" (23:40). While the Bible may indicate that a festival or celebration takes place for seven days, as it does with Sukkot, it is customary for some of these holidays to last longer than seven days outside the Land of Israel because of the complicated issues with the calendar and determining the first day of the month and when the new moon appears. Such is the case with Sukkot, so it is celebrated for eight days.

The plants used in the observance of the holiday are understood as the citron (*etrog,* a lemon-type fruit, which is not very palatable); a palm branch (*lulav*); three sprigs of myrtle leaves; and two sprigs of willow. The *lulav* (a general term that refers to the palm and the attendant myrtle and willow) and the *etrog* are held together during the holiday recital of the *Hallel* Psalms (Psalms 113–118) in the morning worship service, as well as during a processional—which includes the Torah—at which time the *Hoshanah* ("Redemption") prayers are recited.

A special blessing is recited for the shaking of the *lulav* and the *etrog,* said at Sukkot services. There is a specific choreography to the blessing. We take the *lulav* (palm, myrtle, and willow held together) in the right hand, and the fragrant *etrog* in the left. On one end of the *etrog* is a *pitom* (not to be confused with the stem, which is on the opposite end). The blessing is said with the *pitom* held down. Then, after the blessing is recited, the *pitom* is turned upright. The blessing is:

> *Barukh atah Adonai Eloheinu Melekh ha'olam asher
> kid'shanu b'mitzvotav v'tzivanu al n'tilat lulav.*
> Praised are You, Adonai our God, Sovereign of the
> universe, who made us holy by *mitzvot* [command-
> ments] and instructed us to take up the *lulav*.

After the blessing is recited, the *lulav* and the *etrog* are held together and shaken in the six directions of the universe: east, south, west, north, up, and down. (There are a variety of customs as to the order of the directions for shaking.) Many explanations have been offered for the choreography of these rituals. The shaking of the *lulav* and the *etrog* in all directions, for example, may be an act of gathering in the spiritual energy from all the places in the world.

Sukkot Calendar

Because of the eight-day span of the holiday, the first two days are considered holidays, while the five following days take on a hybrid quality, called *Hol Hamoed* ("Middle Days")—not quite holiday, not quite secular. The holiday Torah reading, for example, is shorter during this intermediate period. The last one or two days are also considered holidays (depending on your religious movement): Shemini Atzeret and Simchat Torah, the latter of which is discussed in chapter 4.

The seventh day of Sukkot is Hoshanah Rabbah, which is considered a special day, but not a holiday. Literally translated as the "Great Redemption" and named after the *Hoshanah* ("Redemption") prayers, this holiday has a unique custom associated with it. During the Hoshanah Rabbah service, worshipers use the same four plants required for Sukkot observance, the *lulav* (a general term that refers to the palm and the attendant myrtle and willow) and the *etrog* (a lemon-type fruit, which is not very palatable). With these plants together in one hand, worshipers make seven circuits around the congregation while reciting the *Hoshanot* prayers. After the seven circuits are completed, the worshipers take the willows and beat them on the ground causing some of the leaves to fall off, which symbolizes not only the fragility of the branch, but human frailty as well. We are meant to feel like the willow, which, like most trees, loses its leaves. But, when God sends rain the tree's strength is renewed and it grows new leaves. So too do we "shed leaves"—we lose our strength and struggle at times in our lives—but with faith in God we can be renewed.

Hoshanah Rabbah observance borrows heavily from Yom Kippur symbolism. Because of this close relationship, the leaves that are lost are also meant to symbolize the shedding of our sins from the past year.

Shemini Atzeret is technically a one-day holiday, but is most often thought of as the eighth and last day of Sukkot. The name is from the Bible, which decrees that there should be a solemn gathering (*atzeret*) on the eighth day (*shemini*) after Sukkot begins. It is during this gathering that a prayer for rain is said. The cantor and the rabbi wear white robes or traditional *kittels* (burial shrouds) and the prayers are sung to Yom Kippur melodies, thus beginning Israel's rainy season. We wait to pray for rain after Sukkot so that we will (hopefully) have dry days to sit in our *sukkot* we have built without getting drenched.

Because Shemini Atzeret comes after the High Holidays and Sukkot, Jewish tradition sees the meaning of the holiday as an opportunity to take a deep reflective breath after all the celebration and prayer that has been going on for two weeks, before resuming our normal, day-to-day routines.

Sukkot Blessings

As with nearly all Jewish holidays, the festival of Sukkot is introduced with the lighting of candles and a traditional blessing
over wine called the *Kiddush*. Additionally, a prayer of thanksgiving, which is familiar to many holidays and other occasions,
is also recited. A blessing concerning the act of sitting in a
sukkah is recited as well. Here are the blessings for Sukkot:

Candlelighting

*Barukh atah Adonai Eloheinu Melekh ha'olam asher
kid'shanu b'mitzvotav v'tzivanu l'hadlik ner shel Yom Tov.*
Praised are You, Adonai our God, Sovereign of the
universe, who made us holy by *mitzvot* [command-
ments] and instructed us to light the holiday candles.

Over Wine

*Barukh atah Adonai Eloheinu Melekh ha'olam, borei p'ri hagafen.
Barukh atah Adonai Eloheinu Melekh ha'olam, asher bachar
banu mikol am v'rom'manu mikol lashon v'kid'shanu
b'mitzvotav vatiten lanu Adonai Eloheinu b'ahavah mo'adim
l'simchah chagim uz'manim l'sasson et yom chag haSukkot
hazeh, zeikher litzi'at Mitzrayim.
Ki vanu vacharta v'otanu kidashta mikol ha'amim umo'adei
kodsh'kha b'simcha uv'sasson hinchaltanu.
Barukh atah Adonai, m'kadesh Yisra'eil v'haz'manim.*
Praised are You, Adonai our God, Sovereign of the
universe, who creates fruit of the vine.
Praised are You, Adonai our God, Sovereign of the
universe, who has chosen and distinguished us from all
others by adding holiness to our lives with *mitzvot*
[commandments].

Lovingly have You given us festivals for joy and holidays
for happiness, among them this day of Sukkot, a day of
sacred assembly recalling the Exodus from Egypt.
Thus You have chosen us, endowing us with holiness
from among all peoples by granting us your hallowed
festivals in happiness and joy.
Praised are You, God, who hallows the people
Israel and the festivals.

A Prayer of Thanksgiving

*Barukh atah Adonai Eloheinu Melekh ha'olam shehecheyanu
v'kiymanu v'higi'anu laz'man hazeh.*
Praised are You, Adonai our God, Sovereign of the
universe, who has given us life, sustained us,
and helped us reach this moment.

*Barukh atah Adonai Eloheinu Melekh ha'olam asher
kid'shanu b'mitzvotav v'tzivanu leishev basukkah.*
Praised are You, Adonai our God, Sovereign of the
universe, who made us holy by *mitzvot* [commandments]
and instructed us to dwell in the *sukkah*.

Ushpizin (Guests)

Since hospitality to others is a religious commandment, people
often invite guests into their *sukkot*. It is also customary to
invite the presence of well-known people from the Jewish past
as guests, in particular Abraham, Isaac, Jacob, Joseph, Moses,
Aaron, and David. In the spirit of gender equality, many people
invite the women related to these leaders as well as other
women who led the Jewish people in ancient times: Sarah,
Rebekah, Leah, Rachel, Dinah, Miriam, and Ruth.

Ecclesiastes

On a day during Sukkot, usually on the Sabbath that falls during the holiday, the book of Ecclesiastes, or selections from it, is read, probably because its theme is the harvest of one man's life. Furthermore, the book of Ecclesiastes echoes the theme of temporality. Its best-known phrases, such as "Vanity of vanities, all is vanity" (1:2) and "There is nothing new under the sun" (1:9), reflect our own fleeting natures compared to God, who is eternal. One of Ecclesiastes' most familiar teachings plays on a similar theme:

> To everything there is a season, a time to every purpose under Heaven: a time to be born and a time to die, a time to plant and a time to uproot what has been planted, a time to kill and a time to heal, a time to tear down and a time to build up, a time to weep and a time to laugh, a time of mourning and a time of dancing, a time to throw stones and a time to gather stones, a time to embrace and a time to avoid embracing. There is a time to seek and a time to lose, a time to keep and a time to cast off. There is a time for ripping and a time for sewing. There is a time to be silent and a time to speak. There is a time for love and a time for hate. There is a time for war and a time for peace. (3:1–8)

CHRISTIAN PARALLELS TO SUKKOT

The American Thanksgiving holiday derives from the biblical description of the holiday of Sukkot, known to the Pilgrims as Tabernacles. As Bible readers, the Pilgrims used Sukkot as a model for the Thanksgiving holiday they created. Perhaps it is difficult to find precise religious parallels to Sukkot because the

Catholic Church stamped out the harvest festivals celebrated locally by farmers; the Church perceived them as pagan festivals, antithetical to Catholic practice.

The water libation ceremony that was part of the folk origin of the Sukkot festival—since Sukkot ushered in the rainy season in Israel—parallels customs in many ancient cultures. A Christian remnant of the ancient Temple rite may be found in the Festival of the Cross (*Maskal*), still observed by the Ethiopian Church on September 26.

Although there may be limited parallels to the holiday of Sukkot itself, certain of its symbols are used in Christian tradition. For example, the *Hoshanah* liturgy from Sukkot is repeated in Matthew 21:9. According to Christian Scriptures (Matthew 21:8 and John 12:13), people went out with palm branches to greet Jesus in Jerusalem. It is from this original context that Palm Sunday gets its name and its ritual.

The beating of the willow on Hoshanah Rabbah is similar to "Easter smacks" in spring festivals that are celebrated throughout Europe. Fastelavn, the Monday preceding Ash Wednesday, is a general school holiday and may be considered one of the happiest times of year for schoolchildren. Everybody celebrates the day by eating *Fastelavnsboller*, or Shrovetide buns, which are, generally, sweet buns made with almond stuffing. In some places children take "Lenten birches" (branches decorated with brightly colored paper flowers), get up early in the morning, enter their parents' or grandparents' rooms, and awaken them by beating the bedclothes with their switches while asking for these buns. These noisy smacks probably gave rise to the notion of "Easter smacks," which are delivered in many lands at this season and regarded as part of an early spring purification rite. While they have no ideological relation to the beating of the willow for Hoshanah Rabbah in Judaism, the physical practice looks similar.

There was also a tradition in Old Central Europe during which men and women "beat" each other with birch branches and the so-called payment for the beating was dyed eggs (which were also called Easter smacks); this may have been what gave rise to egg-rolling on Easter. The practice of the beating of the willow is also followed on St. Stephens Day (December 26) and Holy Innocents Day (December 28). In Russia, it was common on Palm Sunday.

4

SIMCHAT TORAH
REJOICING IN THE TORAH

> Be glad and rejoice in Simchat Torah and give honor to
> the Torah ... for she is our strength and our light.
> —FROM A SIMCHAT TORAH SONG

The legs start to get a little tired after the sixth dance. The
calves feel a bit cramped and the feet start to ache, but the
prayer leader calls for another circle dance, so people are roused
to celebrate with full force. Children are dancing on parents'
shoulders or waving flags decorated with the Torah. Someone
is holding the sacred Torah in the middle of the dancing, holding it tightly as a person might hold a newborn—and the circles of dancers move around singing joyfully.

On one day of the year, Jews are instructed to delight
with the Torah. The holiday of Simchat Torah literally means
"joy of Torah." Participating in the joy of Torah on this day
means one thing: dancing. In almost any synagogue you might
attend, the holiday is marked by joyful circle dances around the
Torah. Simchat Torah begins right after Shemini Atzeret ends
(see chapter 3). (In the Reform tradition, Simchat Torah and
Shemini Atzeret are observed on the same day.) Simchat Torah
celebrates the transition from concluding the public reading of
the Torah for one year to immediately beginning the reading
for the following year.

THE BASICS: SIMCHAT TORAH AND JOY

Jews are known as the "people of the book." This idea is given full expression during Simchat Torah, when we celebrate the culmination of the weekly reading of *the* book. The Torah is the heart of Judaism. There is a theological parallel between the Torah in Judaism and Jesus in Christianity. In the beginning of the Gospel of John, the Gospel introduces Jesus as "the word becoming flesh." Just as the Torah is the divine revelation of God's word in Judaism, Jesus is its divine revelation in Christianity. Both Judaism and Christianity are postrevelatory religions. They are religions that begin with an experience of revelation. In one, divine revelation is represented by Torah; in the other, it is represented by Jesus.

Of course, there is an important theological difference between the revelation of words and the revelation of flesh. Christianity emphasizes a relationship with Jesus as a person, while Judaism asks its adherents for something more abstract: to worship a God who is known principally through words. But to get a sense of what is at stake at Simchat Torah, why the celebration is so intense, it is important to understand the centrality of the Torah.

When Jews use the word *Torah,* they often mean more than just the Five Books of Moses, which reflects its technical usage. They may mean the entire Bible; they may mean the words of the Talmud as well (also called the "oral Torah"); they may even mean any Jewish teaching from any period that illuminates something about our existence. The mystical strain of Judaism goes even further to suggest that the Torah is the body of God (a more direct parallel to Christianity, to be sure). It is difficult to articulate exactly what the mystics mean without some background in Jewish mysticism, but there is a sense that the inscribed letters of the Torah themselves are part of the Godhead. That is how central the Torah is to Judaism.

Jews also believe that the Torah represents Jewish continuity from one generation to the next. In some bar mitzvah and bat mitzvah ceremonies (a coming-of-age ritual for a boy or girl at thirteen), the rabbis like to hand the Torah to the parents of the child, who then give it to the child as an expression of the linking of generations. My own synagogue (Dan's), like many in America, has a Torah scroll that was written in Prague in the 1800s and saved from the Holocaust. Although we have other Torah scrolls, we deliberately read from this one at every bar or bat mitzvah to explicitly make the link between generations of Jews. The celebration of Simchat Torah is thus nothing less than the celebration of Jewish life.

My family (Kerry's) actually has two Torah scrolls, designated for each one of our two sons. One came from the mystical city of Safed in Israel. The second was smuggled out of Romania after the Holocaust. We wanted to make sure that the link of Torah between the generations would be clear in our family, and so we use these Torah scrolls at special family celebrations.

As one of the most joyous holidays of the year, Simchat Torah is accompanied by dancing and singing, with the Torah at the center of all the merriment. Because of the celebratory nature of the holiday, only Purim (see chapter 6) compares to its festive atmosphere during the Jewish calendar year. The primary feature of the holiday is a series of seven circuits carrying the Torah, called *hakafot,* which are punctuated by extensive dancing and singing. Children are invited to participate, and often the celebration takes people outside the walls of the synagogue and its sanctuary.

After the dancing, the last section of the Torah is read, in which Moses bids farewell to the People of Israel. This is known as *Vezot Haberachah,* "This is the blessing." It is the only time in which the Torah is read at night. Then the Torah is rolled back to its beginning and the portion designated for the first of the year is read. Anyone who wants the opportunity to do so is given the honor of reading the blessings before and after the Torah reading; this is called an *aliyah* to the Torah and is best described as a Torah honor because it is considered an honor to be involved in a public Torah reading. The last *aliyah* is reserved for children, who are usually permitted to come forward to the Torah during its reading (until they have marked the age of bar mitzvah or bat mitzvah). They stand together under a large tallit (prayer shawl) as the rabbi blesses them following their participation.

HISTORICAL BACKGROUND: THE ORIGIN AND DEVELOPMENT OF SIMCHAT TORAH

The celebration of Simchat Torah probably dates back to the eleventh century in Western Europe, which is quite recent by Jewish standards. It was originally the second day of Shemini Atzeret and was inspired by the annual cycle of assigned public Torah readings.

The ceremony itself is a mystical simulation of a wedding ceremony between Israel and the Torah. The grooms who participate in the Torah reading, as described below, are assisted by groomsmen. Even the seven circuits of the Torah resemble the seven times that a bride encircles the groom during a traditional Jewish wedding ceremony. The customs surrounding the Torah readings also echo the tradition of celebrating with the groom in the synagogue on the Shabbat following his wedding.

SIMCHAT TORAH CUSTOMS AND OBSERVANCES

During the morning service, the Torah honors are given to three honorees who are called grooms (*chattanim*). The first Torah honor goes to the "groom of the Torah" (*chatan Torah*). The second one goes to the "Genesis groom" (*chatan bereshit*), in whose honor the first chapter of Genesis, the story of creation, is read. The last one is called the "groom for the reading of the prophets" (*chatan maftir*), who reads about the succession of leadership from Moses to Joshua. In some congregations, it is customary to try to distract this last groom from his reading, adding to the festive atmosphere of the day. Among liberal congregations, all these roles are played by women as well as men.

During the Torah circuits, it is customary in some communities, such as in Rome, to throw nuts at those in the processional. In other communities, since all the Torah scrolls are taken from the ark, a lighted candle is placed inside the ark so that "the light of Torah should never go out."

Like nearly all Jewish holidays, the festival of Simchat Torah is introduced with the lighting of candles and a traditional blessing over wine called the *Kiddush*. Here are the blessings that are recited:

Candlelighting

Barukh atah Adonai Eloheinu Melekh ha'olam asher kid'shanu b'mitzvotav v'tzivanu l'hadlik ner shel Yom Tov.
Praised are You, Adonai our God, Sovereign of the universe, who made us holy by *mitzvot* [commandments] and instructed us to light the holiday candles.

Over Wine

Barukh atah Adonai Eloheinu Melekh ha'olam, borei p'ri hagafen.
Barukh atah Adonai Eloheinu Melekh ha'olam, asher bachar
banu mikol am v'rom'manu mikol lashon v'kid'shanu
b'mitzvotav vatiten lanu Adonai Eloheinu b'ahavah mo'adim
l'simchah chagim uz'manim l'sasson et yom hashemini,
chag ha-atzeret hazeh, z'man Simchateinu,
mikra kodesh zeikher litzi'at Mitzrayim.
Ki vanu vacharta v'otanu kidashta mikol ha'amim umo'adei
kodsh'kha b'simcha uv'sasson hinchaltanu.
Barukh atah Adonai, m'kadesh yisra'eil v'haz'manim.
Praised are You, Adonai our God, Sovereign of the
universe, who creates fruit of the vine.
Praised are You, Adonai our God, Sovereign of the
universe, who has chosen and distinguished us from all
others by adding holiness to our lives with *mitzvot*
[commandments].
Lovingly have You given us festivals for joy and holidays
for happiness, among them this eighth day Feast of
Assembly, the season of our gladness, a day of sacred
assembly recalling the Exodus from Egypt.
Thus You have chosen us, endowing us with holiness
from among all peoples by granting us your hallowed
festivals in happiness and joy.
Praised are You, God, who hallows the people
Israel and the festivals.

Since Simchat Torah is a synagogue-based holiday, there is no
formal observance of it in the home, except for the holiday
blessings that accompany the meals, as noted above, as on every
holiday. Families with young children may engage in art proj-
ects such as making flags in anticipation of the holidays, which
are then taken to the synagogue to be used during the celebration there.

OTHER SIMCHAT TORAH TEXTS

The final words of the Torah reading for Simchat Torah record the last days of the life of Moses. The haftarah (Joshua 1:1–18), the reading from Prophets, begins where the Torah ends: Joshua assumes the mantle of leadership for himself. Joshua, Moses's chief disciple, represents a continuity of leadership. Part of God's message of initiation to Joshua is included in the following words, which are read aloud:

> Let this book of instruction not cease from your lips; instead recite it day and night, so that you may observe faithfully all that is written in it. Only then will you prosper in your undertakings and only then will you be successful.
>
> (JOSHUA 1:8)

A MODERN SIMCHAT TORAH CELEBRATION

During the 1960s, young Jews in the former Soviet Union began to use the public Torah processionals on Simchat Torah as an opportunity to affirm and celebrate their Jewish identity in public, even if they defined it more in secular than religious ways. The crowds in Moscow and Leningrad (now St. Petersburg) grew into the tens of thousands during this time. The Torah processionals became symbolic of the resistance of Soviet Jews to the repressive Communist regime, particularly when Western visitors participated, as observed by the Western press. Participating in such a ceremony was potentially dangerous, as the Soviet authorities kept track of who attended. Simchat Torah in the former Soviet Union was a unique celebration, in which people risked their lives to celebrate with the Torah. In response, American synagogues began to hold solidarity rallies with Soviet Jews on or near Simchat Torah. Once the walls of the Iron Curtain were torn down, these rallies became part of Jewish memory.

CHRISTIAN PARALLELS TO SIMCHAT TORAH

What is most closely related to Simchat Torah is the lectionary cycle itself, as well as the carrying and presentation of Scriptures during the procession that introduces most Christian worship. The lectionary is a book of Bible passages for reading, study, or preaching in worship services. A lectionary can include readings for weekdays, although the term is more commonly applied today to the Scripture readings for Sundays and holidays. Some churches, such as those in the Roman Catholic and Lutheran tradition, have their own lectionaries, while other churches follow a common, shared lectionary.

Dancing, which is a prominent feature of Simchat Torah, is uncommon in most Roman Catholic and Protestant churches; only in the past few years have Christians incorporated this practice as a way to express joy in the Divine. A primary example is Archbishop Desmond Tutu who dances around the Episcopal altar as part of his traditional South African heritage.

5

HANUKKAH

LIGHTING CANDLES IN
THE DARKNESS

Not by power, not by might, says God.

—ZECHARIAH 4:6

In 1879 a group of young Jews from Philadelphia wanted to revitalize Jewish life. They felt as if Jews had stopped observing their religion, and they were fearful that Judaism would not survive in America. They hit upon a plan to celebrate a minor holiday, which few Jews actually were celebrating in post–Civil War America. The holiday they decided to celebrate was Hanukkah.

It may seem odd that most Jews in America, at one time, did not even celebrate the holiday that is probably now the most well-known Jewish holiday in North America. Hanukkah is considered a so-called minor festival in the Jewish calendar, compared to the other holidays described in this book. It is not mentioned in the Bible, and it does not contain the same Jewish legal prohibitions of doing work as do the other major holidays. Nonetheless, because it falls when Christmas does—and like Christmas, giving gifts is one of its customs—Hanukkah has attained the status of a major holiday in American Jewish life today.

THE BASICS: HANUKKAH AND THE MIRACLE
OF RELIGIOUS FREEDOM

Hanukkah means "rededication." The festival takes its name from the rededication ceremony of the ancient Temple in

Jerusalem, which was defiled by the Assyrian-Greeks in their attempt to Hellenize Jerusalem and Israel. Hanukkah is observed for eight days throughout the Jewish world; part of what the holiday celebrates is the miraculous victory of a small band of Jews over the immense Assyrian-Greek army—those who sought to end Judaism forever.

The well-known myth of the Hanukkah story is that the victors, upon their return to Jerusalem, found the Temple in disrepair and began to clean it only to discover enough consecrated oil to light the lamps for one day. That oil, however, burned for eight days; it lasted long enough to secure more consecrated oil and dedicate the Temple.

While the myth of the oil was relegated to the margins of the Hanukkah story, it emerged as the centerpiece of Hanukkah after the Jewish people placed an overwhelming emphasis on the military victory, rather than the spiritual triumph, that Hanukkah originally commemorated. The placement of this story in the forefront was not just a means by which the Rabbis in the third century could introduce a miracle story into the festival commemoration, nor was it intended to make the holiday more child-friendly. The Rabbis believed that the people had lost the sacred understanding of the festival and sought to elevate it to a higher religious plane.

HISTORICAL BACKGROUND: THE ORIGIN AND DEVELOPMENT OF HANUKKAH

The unfolding of historical events in the ancient Near East provides a backdrop for the miracle story. Alexander the Great had conquered Israel and most of the Near East. When he died in 323 BCE, his empire was divided among his generals, two of whom established their own sovereign kingdoms in Egypt and Syria. Israel, located between these two countries, was valuable to both. As a result, Israel became a battlefield, sometimes ruled by one; sometimes by the other.

In 175 BCE, when Israel was under Syrian control, Antiochus IV (Antiochus Epiphanes IV) became king of Syria. In an effort to strengthen his hold on Israel, he declared that all his subjects must worship the same (Greek) gods and follow the same (Greek) customs. The Jews were not permitted to study Torah, observe Shabbat, or do anything Jewish.

Some Jews, called Hellenists, were enamored of the Greek way of life and fully assimilated into Greek culture. They wore Greek clothing and spoke Greek. Their opponents, called Hasidim (not to be confused with modern Hasidim, who are known by their black coats, fur hats, and *payot,* or earlocks), did not approve of Hellenization. They feared that the influence of Greek culture would destroy Judaism. The Hasidim began their opposition with a simple refusal to obey the laws of Antiochus. As a result, they suffered harshly. They had no choice but to rebel. Beginning in the small town of Modiin, not far from Jerusalem, a priest named Mattathias launched the revolt. He called on others to join him: "Whoever is for God, come with me." The small band of Mattathias and his five sons (who took the name Maccabees, or hammer) began a guerilla offensive in the hills against the mighty Assyrian-Greek army. (The name *Maccabee* was later associated as a word formed from the acronym of the words of the Israelites at the Red Sea: "Who is like You, God, among the gods that are worshiped?") The guerilla offensive deteriorated into a civil war of sorts. Led by one of Mattathias's sons, Judah, this small army liberated Jerusalem. This indeed was a miraculous victory.

The Maccabees cleansed the Temple, then removed the statues of Zeus and the other Greek gods. On the twenty-fifth day of the Hebrew month of Kislev (which usually occurs in December, around the time of the winter solstice, the darkest day of the year, when it is natural to seek light) in the year 165 BCE, they rededicated the Temple. Following the model of Sukkot, which they had not been able to celebrate, the dedication of the Temple lasted for eight days. Slowly, the aspects of the Sukkot celebration in the context of Hanukkah gave way to particular observances reserved for Hanukkah alone.

Hanukkah Customs and Observances

Hanukkah has become the most celebrated of all the holidays on the Jewish calendar. To a large extent it is because of the many customs that illumine our homes alongside the Hanukkah menorah. While many of these customs are influenced by the season, it seems that the holiday lends itself to such customs, as well.

Lighting Candles

Although light is associated with most holidays, it is particularly important to the celebration of Hanukkah. The lights of Hanukkah mark each day of the festival, while serving as reminders of the menorah (candelabra) that burned continuously in the ancient Temple. Using a helper candle (*shammash*) to light them, eight candles are lit in a *hanukkiyah* (Hanukkah menorah/candleholder), starting with one on the first day and adding another each additional day so that eight candles are burning on day eight. Oil with wicks can also be used in *hanukkiyot* (plural of *hanukkiyah*) designed for this purpose. After lighting the candles or wicks, no work is to be done for at least thirty minutes, which is the minimum time that the candles are burning. Here are the blessings that are recited:

On lighting the *hanukkiyah*

[On each night:]
*Barukh atah Adonai Eloheinu Melekh ha'olam asher
kid'shanu b'mitzvotav v'tzivanu l'hadlik ner shel Chanukah.*
Praised are You, Adonai our God, Sovereign of the
universe, who made us holy by *mitzvot* [commandments]
and instructed us to light the Hanukkah candles.

*Barukh atah Adonai Eloheinu Melekh ha'olam, she'asah
nissim la'avoteinu bayamim haheim bazman hazeh.*
Praised are You, Adonai our God, Sovereign of the universe, who performed miracles for our ancestors at this
season in ancient days.

[On the first night only:]
*Barukh atah Adonai Eloheinu Melekh ha'olam shehecheyanu
v'kiymanu v'higi'anu laz'man hazeh.*
Praised are You, Adonai our God, Sovereign of the universe, who has given us life, sustained us, and helped us
reach this moment.

Following the lighting of the candles, a longer section of
text, called *Hanerot Hallalu* ("These Lights"), is recited.

We kindle these lights [*hanerot hallalu*] [to remember] the
miracles, the wonders, the salvations, and the battles which
You performed for our ancestors in former days at this
season through Your holy priest. During these eight days,
these lights are sacred. We are not permitted to use them
for mundane purposes, only to gaze at them [intently] as
a way of thanking You for Your [unending] miracles,
wonders, and salvations.

Sephardic Jews (those who are descended from Spanish
Jews) recite Psalm 30 following the lighting of the candles.

Psalm 30

A Psalm; a Song at the Dedication of the House of David.

I will extol thee, O Adonai, for You have raised me up, and
have not caused my enemies to rejoice over me.

O Adonai, my God, I cried to You, and You healed me.

O Adonai, You brought up my soul from the depths; You
kept me alive, so that I did not go down to the pit.

Sing praise to Adonai, O you God's divine ones, and give
thanks to God's holy reputation.

For God's anger [lasts] only for a moment, God's favor is
for a lifetime; weeping may tarry for the night, but joy
comes in the morning.

Now I had said in my security: "I shall never be moved."

O Adonai, in Your favor, You have established my mountain as a stronghold. [When] You hid Your face, I was
frightened.

Unto You, O Adonai, did I call, and unto Adonai did I
make supplication:

"What profit is there in my blood, when I go down to the
pit? Will the dust praise You? Will it declare Your truth?

Listen, O Adonai, and be gracious to me; Adonai, be my
helper."

For me, You turned my mourning into dancing; You loos-
ened my sackcloth, and strengthened me with gladness;

So that I may sing praises to You, and not be silent; O
Adonai, my God, I will give thanks to You forever.

Playing Dreidel (Spinning Top)

Probably based on a German gambling game, the dreidel game
was adapted to emphasize the miracle of Hanukkah. Each of

the four sides of the dreidel is marked with a Hebrew letter standing for one word in the phrase *Nes Gadol Hayah Sham* ("A Great Miracle Happened There"). Israeli dreidels have a different fourth letter, *peh* for *Poh* ("Here"). Often players use nuts, raisins, or chocolates wrapped in foil to look like coins as gambling tokens.

Taking turns, each person spins the dreidel. Winning or losing is determined by which side of the dreidel is face up when it falls. *Nun* stands for "nothing" (from *nisht* in Yiddish), so the player does nothing. *Gimmel* stands for "all" (*gantz* in Yiddish), so the player takes everything in the pot. *Heh* stands for "half" (*helb* in Yiddish), so the player takes half of what is in the pot. *Shin* (or *peh* on the Israeli dreidel) stands for "put in" (*shtel* in Yiddish), so the player puts one in the pot.

Eating Latkes and Sufganiot

Since the miracle of Hanukkah is associated with oil, various traditions emerged concerning the eating of foods made with or in oil. In Ashkenazic communities, whose members descended from the Germanic lands, potato pancakes (latkes) became the favorite. In many Sephardic families, those descended from Spain—and in Israel—jelly doughnuts fried in oil (*sufganiot*) became the festival food of choice.

Giving Gifts

It is hard to think about Hanukkah today without thinking about giving gifts. Many families have created their own customs when it comes to gift-giving. In some families the custom is to give one gift each night. In others, each night has a different theme. Sometimes these themes are more about giving to the community than about giving gifts to one another. In still other families, different nights are devoted to exchanging gifts with particular relatives.

The giving of gifts on Hanukkah may be more reflective of North American culture than of historical Jewish tradition. The idea of Hanukkah *gelt* ("money" in Yiddish), the core Hanukkah gift, probably grew out of a practice in seventeenth-century Poland when children were given coins and, in turn, gave these coins to their poorly paid teachers as a bonus. Gift-giving at this time of year stems from the connection between the root words for Hanukkah and education (*chinukh* in Hebrew). As communities became more affluent, children were given these same coins to keep for themselves—and share with others. They were encouraged to give some of these coins to charity. Over time, gifts replaced the coins, and it seems we may have forgotten some of the sharing along the way. Some of these customs remain in Jewish communities around the world. When Syria had a larger Jewish community, children frequently received a *chamsa* (a hand-shaped amulet used to ward off evil spirits). And in Turkey, families still share sweets with one another during the extended week of Hanukkah. No matter where the community is located, gift-giving is always inseparable from the celebration.

Other Hanukkah Rituals

There is a special insert added to the core prayer (the *Amidah*, known as the standing prayer, since it is said while standing) in the morning and evening services called *Al Hanissim* (literally, "For these miracles"), as well as in the grace after meals. Both are found in most Jewish prayer books. The *Hallel* Psalms (Psalms 113–118) are also read during the morning service each day throughout the festival.

OTHER HANUKKAH TEXTS

While the main story of Hanukkah is perhaps more well known than some others, there are many side stories that add flavor and substance to the holiday and its celebration. And since sacred texts are the touchstone of Jewish spirituality they raise the celebration to a higher spiritual level especially because of the many customs, such as gift-giving, that threaten to eclipse the holiday's essential message.

Hannah and Her Seven Sons

While the story of Hannah and her seven sons can be found in various places in rabbinic literature, it originally appears in 2 Maccabees and is elaborated upon in 4 Maccabees, both volumes preserved in Christian Bibles. In the original version, an unnamed woman and her sons choose to die at the hands of Antiochus Epiphanes IV rather than submit to the Greek way of life. Through the writing of the Rabbis, this woman is given the name Miriam, and the story is moved from the second century BCE to the second century CE. In the tenth-century *Book of Yosippon,* where the story appears in its original historical context, the woman is named Hannah. Both the Eastern and Western Christian church adopted Hannah and her sons as "Maccabean saints," for whom an annual day of commemoration takes place.

Judith

The story of Judith is told in the collection of books known as the Apocrypha. It tells the tale of Judith and Holofernes, a general who served under Nebuchadnezzar, king of Assyria. Nebuchadnezzar was angry at the people in the western parts of his empire who refused to support his military campaign. So he sent Holofernes and a large army to destroy their local shrines, including those of the Jews in the Land of Israel. While the Jews residing in Israel fortified the mountain passes to Jerusalem, Holofernes attacked the village of Betulia. Judith, a resident of Betulia, left her home in order to befriend, seduce, and then behead Holofernes. When his soldiers learned of his death, they panicked and retreated.

A MODERN HANUKKAH MIRACLE STORY

Associated with the lighting of the candles is the concept of *persumat ha'nes* ("making known the miracle"). This is why the *hanukkiyah* (Hanukkah menorah) is placed where the family gathers so that everyone can witness the miracle. We publicly proclaim the miracle by placing the menorah in the window so that all can see. Some Jews choose to decorate their homes and stencil Hanukkah symbols on the windows. This seems to be what motivated someone to throw a brick through five-year-old Isaac Schnitzer's window on December 2, 1993, during the festival of Hanukkah in Billings, Montana, a city with a tiny Jewish community. Another child's mother, Margaret McDonald, tried to explain what happened by telling her son the story of the Danish people who responded to Hitler's order to the Danish Jews during World War II to identify themselves by wearing yellow Stars of David. The Danish people who were not Jewish put on yellow stars as well, undermining Hitler's intent to segregate and discriminate against the Jews. McDonald persuaded her pastor, the Reverend Keith Torney at the First Congregational United Church of Christ, to ask the Sunday School children to cut out paper menorahs for their own windows. He then persuaded other members of the local clergy to encourage their congregants to do the same thing.

In the weeks that followed, some six thousand homes in Billings, Montana, whose Jewish community numbered only a few dozen families, boasted paper Hanukkah menorahs on their windows, following a decision by the *Gazette* to publish a full-page drawing of a menorah with a general invitation to the residents of Billings to place them on their windows. Although several hate incidents followed—as they had preceding the event in the Schnitzer home—people continued to support one another against baseless hatred. And in the years that followed, Christian families around town continued to place these paper menorahs on their windows in a show of solidarity with the small Jewish community in Billings.

CHRISTIAN PARALLELS TO HANUKKAH

Many people think that Hanukkah and Christmas are paired together in North America only because of the calendar. However, both emerge from a similar religious response to the winter solstice: lighting lights. In Christianity, this light took a path through Germany, where fir trees were adorned with lights to ward off the evil spirits; in Judaism the path went through the menorah of the ancient Temple and then eventually emerged as the Hanukkah menorah, which helps to recall the event that reclaimed and rededicated that Temple. Just as Hanukkah candles mark the eight days it took to dedicate the ancient Temple, Advent candles mark the four weeks of waiting for the coming of the Christ Child. John 10:22 even mentions that Jesus celebrated Hanukkah.

6

PURIM
MERRY-MAKING FOR A
STORY OF REDEMPTION

The days on which the Jews had rest from their enemies,
and the month which was turned for them from sorrow
to gladness, and from mourning into a good day; that they
should make them days of feasting and gladness, and of
sending portions one to another, and gifts to the poor.
—ESTHER 9:22

Purim is the most joyous and raucous of festivals in the Jewish
calendar. It is noted for rather unusual customs which inten-
tionally undermine the piety that accompanies other Jewish
observances. Some of the rituals associated with Purim are
observed in reverse; even the festive meal that begins most
holidays—including the meal that introduces the Yom Kippur
fast—is instead at the end of the Purim festival, when we bid
farewell to its observance. Purim usually falls near the beginning of spring, and those who celebrate Purim let loose the
emotions that have been pent up all year long (especially during winter for those who live in cold climates).

THE BASICS: PURIM AND THE MIRACLE
OF SURVIVAL

The festival of Purim celebrates the successful overthrow of
a plot to destroy the Jewish community of ancient Persia

(modern-day Iran) in the fifth century BCE, as recounted in the storyline in the book of Esther.

The story of Purim, as recounted in the biblical scroll of Esther, recalls King Ahashuerus expelling his queen, Vashti, for refusing to come to a banquet to dance in front of his drunken friends, who had already been partying for six months and were in the midst of an extended weeklong banquet. The entire celebration was initiated to celebrate the third year of Ahasuerus's reign. Following Vashti's expulsion, the king invited Esther, the niece of a nobleman named Mordecai who raised her, to enter the king's harem so she might become his queen. But Esther's Jewish identity was kept secret.

Years later Mordecai was instrumental in uncovering a plot to kill the king. While it was Mordecai who exposed the plot, Haman was charged with investigating the crime. The successful investigation led to Haman's elevation to the post of prime minister. Since Haman was now second only to the king, he wanted the subjects of the king to likewise bow down to him. Mordecai's refusal to do so incensed Haman, prompting him to seek to destroy the entire Persian Jewish community, of which Mordecai (and Esther) were part. The king gave permission for Haman to proceed, but before he could carry out his evil plot, Esther intervened, risking her life by revealing her own Jewish identity. Eventually, the king relented and Haman was hanged on the gallows intended for Mordecai and the other Persian Jews.

The name *Purim* comes from the word for "lots" or "marked stones." The folk explanation for the name emerges from the decision of Haman, the villain in the story, to cast lots to arbitrarily choose the date on which to annihilate the Jewish people who lived in ancient Persia, where he served as vizier to King Ahashuerus. The king is usually identified with Xerxes, although there were several kings with the same name. The word *purim* is also related to the ancient Persian word for "first," a fitting term if the festival is related to the ancient Persian New Year, a suggestion made by some scholars looking for historical precedents for the festival.

Purim is celebrated, in most places, on the fourteenth of the Hebrew month of Adar, following the day that Haman had planned to destroy the Jews of Persia. Instead, the king hanged Haman and allowed the Jews to defend themselves (since his decree against them could not be rescinded once it had been issued, according to the story). The Jews of the ancient Persian capital of Shushan fought back for two days; this second day is called *Shushan Purim* and is part of the explanation as to why, in some places, Purim is celebrated on the fifteenth of Adar. The Rabbis chose to make a distinction between the Persian capital, Shushan, and everywhere else in accordance with the original event. However, the Rabbis did not want to leave out the Land of Israel and give another location special recognition. So they determined that although Shushan at the time was not surrounded by a wall, all cities which were surrounded by a wall in the days of Joshua would be given the same preeminence as Shushan.

In a leap year (when a second month of Adar is added), Purim is celebrated during the second Adar. In those years, the fourteenth of Adar 1 is called *Purim katan* (literally, "small Purim").

HISTORICAL BACKGROUND: THE ORIGIN AND DEVELOPMENT OF PURIM

The historical veracity of the events surrounding the Purim story have been challenged by numerous scholars. Most likely, the festival has its origins in a folk celebration that includes elements that reflect themes similar to those in the Purim celebration: the selection of a new queen—Esther; the parading of a commoner as the king—Mordecai; a fast; and the execution of a felon—Haman. Moreover, the festival is probably related to the time of the vernal equinox, usually in early March, the same time as the old Persian New Year's celebration. Ancient New Year's celebrations usually included a combative battle between two forces (usually good and evil) and the giving of gifts, two of the salient elements in the Purim story. As was common in many cases, these elements of folk religion were absorbed into the Purim story and celebration as the Rabbis sought to incorporate them through Purim into Jewish history and religion.

PURIM CUSTOMS AND OBSERVANCES

The custom of drinking on Purim is probably the most well known tradition that undermines traditional Jewish observance of the holidays, much to the Rabbis chagrin—even though they initiated it. Instead of drinking a small amount of wine as is the custom at most Jewish holidays, there is a tradition of drinking much more than is considered a "normal" share. In place of decorum at religious services, worshipers make huge amounts of noise with really loud instruments whenever one of the heroes or villains of the Purim story is mentioned. Rather than speaking reverently of religious leaders, they are lampooned. Even the liturgy is recited in ways that would otherwise seem inappropriate.

The central part of the Purim celebration is the somewhat raucous reading of the Scroll of Esther. This scroll—referred to as *Megillat Esther*—is read in the synagogue with special cantillations (a system of musical notes for chanting, usually referred to as *trope* in Yiddish or *taamei hamikrah* in Hebrew) during the morning and evening worship services. The scroll of Esther is spread out like a letter for reading. When the verses that relate the survival of the Jewish community are chanted, they are read in a louder voice. When Haman's name is read, listeners try to block out his name by making noise, generally using a Purim noisemaker called a *grogger* (in Yiddish) or *raashan* (in Hebrew). This follows the instruction in Deuteronomy 20 to blot out the name of Amalek, who is allegedly an ancestor of Haman. When the names of Haman's sons are read, they are read in one breath to demonstrate that they were killed together. This also expresses the Jewish value that it is inappropriate to gloat over the misfortune of anyone, even one's enemy.

These blessings are recited before the reading of *Megillat Esther*:

Barukh atah Adonai Eloheinu Melekh ha'olam asher kid'shanu b'mitzvotav v'tzivanu al mikra megillah.
Praised are You, Adonai our God, Sovereign of the universe, who made us holy by *mitzvot* [commandments] and instructed us to read the *megillah*.

Barukh atah Adonai Eloheinu Melekh ha'olam, she'asah nissim la'avoteinu bayamim haheim bazman hazeh.
Praised are You, Adonai our God, Sovereign of the universe, who performed miracles for our ancestors at this season in ancient days.

Barukh atah Adonai Eloheinu Melekh ha'olam shehecheyanu v'kiymanu v'higi'anu laz'man hazeh.
Praised are You, Adonai our God, Sovereign of the universe, who has given us life, sustained us, and helped us reach this moment.

It is also customary to give the equivalent of a half-shekel (a small Hebrew coin) to the poor prior to the reading of the *megillah*. This has been expanded to encompass undertaking general acts of charitable giving prior to the festival. Also related to this tradition is the custom of giving baskets of fruits and pastries to friends for Purim, called *mishloach manot.* Both of these customs are derived from the text of Esther that introduces this chapter.

The establishment of Purim as a feast is noted in the book of Esther (9:20–28). There are a variety of foods associated with this holiday; most of them reflect important elements of the story. Best known among these foods are *hamantaschen,* triangle-shaped pastry pockets that are said to look like the hat that Haman wore. The origins of these pastries are European and probably take their name from a Yiddish wordplay on *man* (poppy seed filling)—as in Haman (the villain)—and *taschen* (pockets). In Israel, the same pastries are called *oznei Haman* (Hebrew for the "ears of Haman").

Other Purim Rituals

Purim holds a most unusual place in Jewish life. The rituals associated with Purim are things which Jews normally do not do in a synagogue. Going to a Purim service can feel in some synagogues like going to a Halloween party. Wearing costumes, shaking loud noisemakers, even drinking alcohol—all of this, of course, is not done the rest of the year. But on Purim these actions are encouraged.

Some Jewish thinkers have seen in Purim frivolities a hint of deeper meaning. To understand this, we need to look again at the Purim story itself. In the Purim story, there is one important character missing from the story. Esther and Mordecai save the Jewish people from Haman. We have the noble hero and heroine and the archetypal bad guy, but one very crucial character is missing who usually has a lot to say in the Bible. God is not mentioned at all in the Book of Esther. God is potentially alluded to when Mordecai says that relief and deliverance will come to the Jews from a different place if Esther chooses not to help (Esther 4:14). But other than this enigmatic phrase, God's name is not mentioned once. It is interesting to note that Judaism celebrates this story of miraculous redemption, yet God is not mentioned as authoring the miracle; it is the people who bring about the redemption for themselves.

Jewish commentators see this story not as a celebration of human power, but rather as an example of God's subtle ways in working through people. Jewish tradition sees God as creating the miracle of Purim through the intervention of Esther, even though God is never mentioned. Just as people wear masks on Purim to look like someone else, so too, perhaps, does God wear a mask. The strange frivolity of Purim may be a hint to us to look for God in places where God is not evident.

The freewheeling celebration of Purim presents some people with real challenges to participation. Many of the so-called values in Purim may seem initially irreverent and inappropriate, unless they are examined more deeply. For example, Vashti exhibited personal courage when she refused to dance for the king's inebriated friends. But the biblical text considers her act as insubordination. Even the so-called beauty contest that Esther entered to be chosen as the next queen suggests that women should be valued for their beauty alone. Finally, the complete destruction of Haman's family—as recorded at the end of the scroll—is certainly not something that we want to suggest as a model of moral living.

Purim parties are often called *adloyadah*, from the phrase *ad d'lo yadah*, "until one does not know," referring to the questionable—but again sanctioned—practice of drinking until we do not know the difference between "Blessed be Mordecai"— the hero of Purim—and "Cursed be Haman"—the villain.

In celebration of the holiday, people dress up in the costume of the characters of the story. The actions of the characters provide the backdrop for the many pageants and plays that are popular expressions of Purim celebration. These plays, which make sanctioned fun of religious leaders, in particular, are known as *Purimshpiels*. Some communities developed their own Purim celebrations. In Provence, for example, the Jewish community elected a Purim king until the Jews were expelled (in 1406) and took the practice to Italy. Later, so-called Purim rabbis were appointed at seminaries and Jewish educational institutions throughout Europe. They would "rule" from the beginning of the Hebrew month of Adar until Purim. This practice was replaced in the United States and elsewhere by a beauty contest for Queen Esther.

Jews have undertaken the practice of fasting for two primary reasons: for self-reflection and as a sign of contrition in an effort to change the will of God. Thus, when Esther and the ancient Jews of Persia fasted (Esther 4:15–16), they were doing so with the hope that God would intervene and change what they saw as their fate. In recognition of the ancient fast, Jews continue the practice of fasting the day before Purim. This fast is called *taanit Esther,* the fast of Esther.

OTHER PURIMS

Following the pattern of the Bible, there are also other commemorations referred to as *Purim* on various dates in local communities. These denote Jewish communities that survived destruction and annihilation, like the Jews of ancient Persia. Unlike other commemorations in the Jewish calendar, these other Purims can actually be marked on days that are already set aside for other holiday or Sabbath observances. Often families saved from certain danger instituted their own personal Purims. While there are hundreds of special communal Purims, many have been forgotten or have disappeared in the course of time. Others are recalled only in community annals and in history books.

CHRISTIAN PARALLELS TO PURIM

While the meaning and the message are far different, formal Purim plays find their analog in the "mysteries" presented in the churches at the Feast of Corpus Christi and at Shrove Tuesday (the day before Ash Wednesday, which is the first day of Lent), as well as the revels of the Twelfth Night. (The Twelfth Night is commemorated on January 5, or January 6 in some communities. It is the twelfth night after Christmas, which marks the end of the season, the epiphany celebration, and the adornment of the Magi.) Even the traditional Twelfth Night mummeries (originally silent folk dramas, which may have celebrated the death of the year and the resurrection of spring) in the Eifel district in Germany deal with retribution against thieves, in a fashion similar to the Purim play's treatment of Haman. The custom of appointing a Purim king or rabbi is similar to the Lords and Abbots of Misrule, the Bishops and Archbishops of Fools, and the Mock Popes, characteristics of the clerical revels of Carnival and the Twelfth Night. In France, the sham pontiff was attired in buffoonery, and in England, the Boy Bishop held office from St. Nicholas Day (December 6) until the Feast of the Holy Innocents (December 28). The prince of the Carnival is also fairly common, especially to the Shrovetide celebrations in Germany. The burning of Haman in effigy finds its parallel in the burning of the straw figure of the Holly Boy in Kent and a puppet known as Ivy Girl. The latter takes the form of Frau Holle in Germany. And in Tudor England, the Twelfth Night marked the end of a winter festival that started on All Hallows Eve (now celebrated as Halloween). A king would be appointed to run the festivities and the normal order of things was reversed, resonant of the way the festival celebration of Purim unfolds.

Since Ash Wednesday (a day of penitence) introduces Lent and its traditional abstinence from eating meat, it gave rise to the need to eat up fats that wouldn't last during Lent; hence Fat Tuesday (*Mardi Gras* in French). This day took on a freewheeling celebratory nature, similar to that of Purim in spirit, because it prefaces a day of introspection with a day of free-spirited revelry. However, Purim does not introduce a religious season, as does Shrove/Fat Tuesday. In many countries, this day is the last day of Carnival. And the Carnival itself mimics the masquerade parties and balls that have marked Purim throughout the centuries.

Furthermore, the Fathers of the Church considered Esther as a type of Blessed Virgin Mary. She becomes the queen who intercedes for the needs of Christians, as in the Cana wedding of John 2. And since Purim includes costumes, painted faces, noisemakers, and good-natured fun, it may also bear a resemblance to those aspects of the celebration of Easter.

7

PESACH

CELEBRATING THE JOURNEY FROM SLAVERY TO FREEDOM

And the blood on the houses where you are staying shall
be a sign for you; when I see the blood I will *pass over* you,
so that no plague will destroy you when I strike the land
of Egypt.

—EXODUS 12:13

In the first of the Ten Commandments, God says, "I am
Adonai your God who brought you out of Egypt" (Exodus
20:2). Some Jewish commentators have asked why God
includes the reference to leaving Egypt. Couldn't God have
just said, "I am Adonai your God" and stopped right there?
The answer lies in the singular importance of God's redemption of Israel from the slavery in Egypt. Crucial to God's relationship with the Jewish people from biblical times until today
is the Exodus from Egypt. The redemption from Egypt is the
ultimate paradigm of freedom and hope in Judaism. This optimism is perhaps among Judaism's greatest gifts to the world.
The leading of the People of Israel from slavery to freedom
becomes enshrined in Judaism's commitment to freedom.
God's parting of the Red Sea to save the Israelites from certain
disaster is the symbol of hope in our darkest hour. The Passover
holiday is a celebration of both freedom and hope.

THE BASICS: PASSOVER AND FREEDOM

Passover reminds Jews to be grateful for the freedom that they have and to truly seek freedom for others. Freedom can take on many different forms, and part of the Passover holiday is often given over to expounding the various meanings of freedom. For some people, freedom means being free from political tyranny. For others, it means freedom from economic desperation. For still others, it may mean freedom from spiritual depression. On Passover, Jews are meant to think about and take action to liberate ourselves and others from all of types of slavery. Passover is also a reminder that however dark a situation may appear, there is the possibility of light and redemption. Judaism is a religion of hope despite darkness. The Passover holiday commemorates this hope and seeks to keep this hope alive for everyone who shares in its celebration.

The other major theme of the holiday is remembering. Passover is, in fact, the only holiday in the Bible where the Jewish community is explicitly told to pass the meaning of the holiday down to our children. In Exodus 13:6–8, God directs as follows, "Seven days you shall eat unleavened bread, and on the seventh day there shall be a festival of Adonai.... And you shall explain to your child on that day, 'It is because of what Adonai did for me when I went forth from Egypt.'" The Bible itself requires members of the Jewish community to value memory; Jews are religiously obligated to tell their children this age-old story to keep its memory alive. As the Baal Shem Tov, the founder of Hasidism, said, "Forgetfulness leads to exile, while memory is the secret of redemption."

HISTORICAL BACKGROUND: THE ORIGIN AND DEVELOPMENT OF PASSOVER

The origins of the holiday are found in the story of the Exodus from Egypt. At the beginning of the book of Exodus, the Israelites have been living in Egypt as slaves for four hundred years. God hears their groaning and, remembering the covenant made with Abraham, Isaac, and Jacob, determines to free Israel through God's emissary Moses. Moses goes before Pharaoh and demands that Pharaoh "Let my people go!" Pharaoh refuses and nine plagues are inflicted on Egypt. The final, tenth, plague is the death of all the firstborn of Egypt.

In Exodus 12, the directive for the holiday is given just before the plague of the firstborn is enacted. In this chapter, God instructs the Israelites to sacrifice a lamb on the twilight of the fourteenth day of the month of Nisan. After the sacrifice that night, they are to eat the lamb with bitter herbs and unleavened bread. The blood of the sacrificed lamb is to be put on the lintels of the doorposts of the houses as a sign for the angel of death to *pass over* (hence the generally accepted origin for the name of the holiday as Passover in English) the Israelites' houses. The Bible instructs the Israelites to practice this ritual of slaughter and feasting on a lamb every year. It also ordains a seven-day festival on which Jews should not eat leavened bread or even have it in their homes.

Historically, after the Israelites settled in the Land of Israel, the holiday changed so that the sacrifice needed to occur at the Temple in Jerusalem. Passover, like Shavuot and Sukkot, is one of the *shalosh regalim,* three pilgrimage holidays, where Israelites were expected to go to Jerusalem to worship. Pilgrims would sacrifice a lamb on the afternoon of the fourteenth of the Hebrew month of Nisan and eat it as part of a ritual meal that evening. This is recorded in the Gospels prior to Jesus's crucifixion, when he travels with his disciples to Jerusalem for the Passover festival. After the destruction of the second Temple in 70 CE, the holiday changed significantly again. No longer were sacrifices practiced; prayer took its place. The focus of the holiday turned to the seder (feast) and the telling of the Exodus story from the *haggadah,* a text used in the celebration to guide the telling at the story.

Much scholarly effort has been focused on determining the precise origins of the seder and the *haggadah. Seder* literally means "order" and refers to the entire first evening of Passover, when Jews come together to retell the story of Passover and eat a festive meal. However, there can be more than one seder during Passover. *Haggadah* means "the telling" and refers to a book that is read by everyone together at the seder. The *haggadah* has songs and rituals, and at its center is a retelling of the Passover story along with a number of interpretations of the story. Scholars suggest that the origins of the *haggadah* were found after the destruction of the Temple in 70 CE. But there are aspects of the *haggadah* that have been added over the centuries, even up to today.

Although it may seem surprising, the origins of the seder may have been significantly influenced by Greek culture. Upper-class Greek men attended symposia—evenings where they reclined on couches, dipped vegetables in sauces, and debated important topics. At the Passover seder, we dip vegetables in sauces, are told to recline at the table, and debate the topic of freedom. It would not be the first time that Judaism has appropriated an aspect of foreign culture and remade it as Jewish. The dipping of vegetables is "made Jewish" by being included in one of the "four questions" that the youngest child at the seder asks. All the questions are about why the Passover night is different from all other nights. The seder is set up in some ways to spur children to ask questions so as to generate debate. Maimonides, the great medieval Jewish philosopher, says that we must do something different from what is done the rest of the year, such as removing the table before people have a chance to eat (a practice not generally followed), so as to elicit a question from the children.

The reclining on couches also becomes transformed in the Jewish seder. Many people bring comfortable pillows to the seder table on which to rest. The tradition is that reclining on pillows is a sign of freedom and of royalty. Slaves would not be able to eat slowly and luxuriate over their meals, so on the night dedicated to freedom, we should bask in that freedom by reclining on pillows.

PASSOVER CUSTOMS AND OBSERVANCES

The many nuanced customs, especially those connected to the seder meal, add to the important lessons that are taught during observance of Passover.

Matzah

Matzah is the unleavened bread that Jews are directed to eat during Passover: "Seven days you shall eat unleavened bread; on the very first day you shall remove leaven from your house" (Exodus 12:15). Matzah is eaten as a symbol of the haste in which the Jews left Egypt. After the tenth plague, the Israelites quickly gathered their things and left Egypt. They didn't have time to allow their bread to rise. Thus, on Passover, we eat matzah, "unrisen" bread, to symbolize this hurry.

Technically, matzah is a mix of flour and water that contains no yeast. The Rabbis determined that from the moment the flour and water are mixed, the entire cooking process must take fewer than eighteen minutes so the bread will not rise. Matzah has spiritual significance as well. It is a symbol of humility and the rejection of arrogance. Just as bread rises, so human beings become "puffed up" and arrogant if we do not consciously guard against this. The flat matzah bread is a reminder of our need to be humble and wary of the human inclination toward arrogance.

There is a moment during the Passover seder when matzah also represents poverty. We say at the seder, "This is the bread of poverty that our ancestors ate in the land of Egypt. Let all who are hungry come and eat, let all who are in need come and share the Passover meal." Matzah here symbolizes both freedom and poverty. It reminds us that we were slaves and also that we should now be grateful for our freedom. There is a custom of inviting guests to the seder, and it is considered especially meritorious to invite those who are poor and in need of food. Danny Siegel, a well-known Jewish writer and poet, recalls that every year his parents would invite severely brain-damaged children whom they did not know—living in a local institution—to his family's seder. Passover is a time to invite others into your home, and they took this commandment to heart. On top of cooking for mountains of guests, Siegel recalls that his parents took the time to do this good deed, and that has made all the difference in his life. It gave him an example of openness and graciousness that he has tried to emulate throughout his life.

Bedikat Chametz (Checking for Leavened Products)

Not only is there a commandment to eat matzah during Passover, there is also a commandment to remove all products containing leavened grains from the home (leavened products are called *chametz*). This means any baked goods, breads, or crackers—most of what you might have in your pantry at any one time. There is a ritual performed the night before Passover, called *bedikat chametz,* "searching for leavened grains." After we have cleaned the entire house and disposed of the *chametz,* we go through the dark house by candlelight (or flashlight) with a feather used as a duster, and a wooden spoon for collecting the last symbolic bits of *chametz*. We then burn the crumbs and the feather and the wooden spoon the following morning. It is a custom in Kerry's family, as it is in many families, to use the *lulav* from their celebration of Sukkot as part of this fire—in order to connect the celebration of one holiday to another.

A practice developed of removing the *chametz* (crackers, cereal, and the like) from the home by gathering all the products that contain the *chametz* and symbolically "selling" them to a non-Jewish neighbor, even though they never leave the house. The practice among most contemporary Jews is to put all the *chametz* in a room or in a closet and then keep the door shut for the entire Passover holiday, so it is as if that place were not part of the home. Often synagogues will facilitate selling the *chametz* to non-Jews who "buy" it for the eight days and then "return" it after Passover, even though the products never leave the closet.

The Haggadah

The *haggadah* is the "script" from which Jews read at the seder. It contains the order of the evening, directions for the rituals performed that night, blessings for the meal, psalms, children's songs for Passover, and, most important, the telling of the Exodus story. The *haggadah* tells the story, however, in a rather unusual manner. Rather than simply quoting the story from Exodus, it quotes verses from other parts of the Bible. The retelling starts with Deuteronomy 26:5–18, which begins, "My father was a wandering Aramean; he went down to Egypt and lived there in small numbers." The *haggadah* then interprets these verses, interweaving stories from later Jewish tradition with the biblical verses. This mode of storytelling is consistent with the Jewish love of interpretation, even at the expense of straightforward clarity.

As mentioned above, the earliest elements in the *haggadah* probably date back to just after the destruction of the Temple in the year 70 CE. But the *haggadah* continued to evolve. Some Passover songs, like *Had Gadya* (Aramaic for "Just One Kid"), are from the fifteenth or sixteenth century. Even today elements are being added and new *haggadot* (plural of *haggadah*) are being written. Today there are a variety of *haggadot* that center on a particular theme and tell the story of Passover to reflect that theme. There are feminist *haggadot,* a vegetarian *haggadah,* a new-age *haggadah,* and so on. You name it, there is a *haggadah* for you.

The Seder Plate

In the center of the Passover table is the seder plate. On the plate is matzah, as well as the following items:

maror—bitter herbs, which symbolize the bitterness of the Israelite slaves' lives

charoset—a sweet mix of wine, nuts, and raisins, symbolizing the mortar the Israelite slaves used

an egg—to symbolize rebirth

karpas—parsley or celery to symbolize spring

a shank bone of a lamb (a roasted beet can be used by vegetarians)—a reminder of the Passover sacrifice that used to occur when the Temple stood.

As with the *haggadah,* there is an ongoing evolution in Passover symbolism, and one of the new items that has appeared on some seder plates recently is an orange. It is attributed to Professor Susannah Heschel, a well-known Jewish feminist, who wanted to put something new on the seder plate to keep solidarity with gay Jewish men and women, as well as others who are marginalized by Jewish society.[1] Some people say the orange represents something different. They tell the story of a man who interrupted a lecture that Professor Heschel was giving to say that a woman becoming a rabbi is as unnatural as an orange on a seder plate. The story is untrue, but many Jewish feminists have kept the orange on the seder plate in honor of women becoming rabbis. (Women can be ordained as rabbis only in the non-Orthodox movements of Judaism—Conservative, Reform, and Reconstructionist.)

While most *sedarim* take place in the home, some synagogues sponsor a community-wide seder, often on the second night of the holiday to allow friends and families to gather in homes on the first night. In addition, worship services with special Torah readings (during morning services) for Passover take place in the synagogue throughout the holidays, according to the tradition of the individual synagogue.

The Four Children

In the *haggadah,* we read about four children. According to the *haggadah* there are four types of children: the wise, the wicked, those of less than average intelligence, and those who do not know how to ask a question. These four children become the source of endless commentary about human nature. The wise children, the *haggadah* tells us, are wise because they ask about the meaning of the Passover laws that God has given us. The wicked children are so called because they ask what Passover has to do with *you.* The *haggadah* instructs us that the source of these children's wickedness is in their failure to identify with the events of the Exodus. By asking, what does this have to do with *you?* rather than, what does this have to do with *us?* the wicked children exclude themselves from the Jewish community as a whole.

The children of less than average intelligence are not interested in a complicated answer or are not able to grasp the sophisticated nuances of abstract ideas. And finally, others are simply too young to even ask the appropriate questions, let alone understand any answers they may be given.

Some commentaries on the *haggadah* turn the four categories around and say that the "wicked" child is actually just provocative, while the wise child lacks humility. Some see the child who does not know how to ask as occupying the highest spiritual realm—beyond words. And some totally reject the idea of children as either wicked or good and see aspects of the four children in all of us. At times we feel of less than average intelligence. At times we are stunned into silence. At times we say the wrong thing. And at times we are wise.

The Ten Plagues

During the Passover seder it is a custom to take one drop of wine for each plague and spill it onto your plate. Although some people contend that the spilling of drops reflects our appreciation for God's judgment against a cruel enemy, most Jews understand the spilling of drops to be in sympathy for the pain of the Egyptians who died during the redemption of the Israelites. As we drop wine from the cup, our own joy is diminished. The Talmud includes a famous story of the Israelites successfully crossing the Red Sea, while their Egyptian pursuers are drowning, "When the angels tried to sing songs of praise to God at the Red Sea, God silenced them, saying, 'My handiwork, my human creatures, are drowning in the Sea, and you want to sing songs of praise?'" (Babylonian Talmud, *Megillah* 10b).

The Afikoman

Afikoman is derived from a Greek word meaning "after procession," used to describe a special piece of matzah hidden away near the beginning of the seder by one of the adults and searched for toward the end of the seder by the children. Whoever finds it is given a prize. After the finding and eating of the *afikoman*, there is no more eating of food at the seder. The *afikoman* is a substitute for the sacrificed lamb that was commanded to be the last thing eaten on Passover night when sacrifices still occurred.

The Four Cups of Wine

During the Passover seder, participants drink four cups of wine. Since the seder lasts many hours, the intention is not to become intoxicated by drinking wine quickly. Instead, the slow consumption of this much wine is a symbol of the freedom of the holiday. One explanation for the four cups of wine is that they represent the four different expressions of redemption that God promises to the Israelites while they are enslaved. In Exodus 6:6–7, God says, "I will free you ... and deliver you.... I will redeem you ... and take you to be My people." There have been recent attempts to add a fifth cup of wine to the seder. When Jews were oppressed in the former Soviet Union, a fifth cup was added to the seder to commemorate the plight of Soviet Jews. Some people add a fifth cup to remember those Jews who were killed in the Holocaust.

The Cup of Elijah

Somewhere on the seder table is a special cup called the cup of Elijah. Toward the end of the Passover seder, one of the participants opens up the door to welcome the prophet Elijah. According to Jewish tradition, Elijah will be the one to herald the coming of the messiah. At every Jewish baby-naming ceremony, there is also a seat for Elijah in hopes that the baby being named brings about Elijah's presence. The opening of the door for Elijah on Passover is a symbol of hope. The seder draws to a close with a vision of Elijah as a hope for a better world, despite whatever is going on around us. Rabbi Judah Loew, also known as the Maharal, a medieval leader of the Jewish community in Prague, wrote the following prayer for Elijah, "May the Merciful One [God] send Elijah the prophet to announce good news about redemption and comfort—just as You promised: 'Here I will send you Elijah the Prophet before Adonai's great and awesome day. God will reconcile the hearts of parents to their children and children to their parents'" (Malachi 3:23–24).

Many Jews have recently added a feminist parallel to Elijah's cup, called Miriam's cup. According to Rabbinic legend, Miriam was responsible for a miraculous well of water that followed the Israelites during their forty-year wanderings in the desert (*Song of Songs Rabbah* 4:12). To recall that Miriam's merit ensured that the Israelites had fresh water in the wilderness, water is placed in a ceremonial Miriam's cup. Some Jews also change the traditional wording of a song for Elijah to include verses about Miriam.

CHRISTIAN PARALLELS TO PASSOVER

Perhaps no other holiday in this book prompts as much comparison with a Christian holiday as Passover does with Easter. The Christian Bible makes several explicit links between Jesus's Last Supper and a Passover seder. Mark 14:12, for example, says that Jesus prepared for the Last Supper on the "first day of Unleavened Bread [Passover] when they sacrificed the Passover lamb." And Paul equates Jesus's crucifixion with the Passover sacrifice, "Our Paschal lamb, Christ has been sacrificed. Therefore let us celebrate the festival, not with the old yeast, the yeast of malice and evil, but with the unleavened bread of sincerity and truth" (1 Corinthians 5:7–8).

Not surprisingly then, the celebration of Easter, commemorating Christ's resurrection, carries many of Passover's themes. They are both spring holidays of renewal, with an emphasis on the overcoming of death itself. The story of Passover has at its heart the Exodus story of the Israelites sacrificing the lamb and putting its blood on the lintel of each doorway to save Israel from the angel of death. The Jews are saved once more from certain death by God's parting of the Red Sea to save Israel from the oncoming chariots of Pharaoh. Passover has as its core the saving power of God over death. Similarly, Easter has as its predominant theme resurrection, God's power over death.

The only problem with this analysis is that there is much debate about whether the Last Supper actually was a Passover seder. While three of the Gospels (Matthew, Mark, and Luke—known collectively as the synoptic Gospels) all agree that the Last Supper was a seder, the Gospel of John does not record any last meal at all and says that Jesus died just before the holiday of Passover began. Scholars disagree as to which Gospel to believe. There is evidence to suggest that the Last Supper was a seder, including the fact that Jesus teaches about the meaning of the symbols of bread and wine present at the Last Supper, similar to a seder, where Jews read about symbolic interpretations of bread, herbs, and the Passover sacrifice. On the other hand, there are scholars who suggest that the Last Supper could not possibly have been a seder, because that would have meant that Jesus's trial and execution would have been carried out during Passover, an unlikely prospect because

Jews would not have taken part in any legal proceedings during the holiday.

The controversy over whether the Last Supper was a seder has historical dimensions as well. The Quartodecimans (the Fourteeners) were early Christians who believed that the date of Easter should be calculated so as to coincide with the Jewish celebration of Passover, whether or not that day was a Sunday. Because the Jewish calendar is primarily a lunar calendar, Passover is always on the fourteenth of Nisan, the new moon, which is not always a Sunday. The Quartodecimans believed in celebrating Easter the night of the fifteenth of Nisan no matter when it fell during the week, so that the connection between the seder/Last Supper and Easter would always be apparent.

We should note that, historically, Christian-Jewish tensions were exacerbated around Passover and Easter, making this a time of heightened danger for Jews. Some scholars claim that the first charge of deicide against the Jews (the assertion that the Jews killed Jesus, and thus that the Jews are eternally responsible for this sin) was brought by Melito of Sardis in the second century CE in a famous sermon called the "Homily on Passover." The charge of deicide was, and in some circles remains, the most divisive issue separating Jews from Christians. Passion plays performed during the holy week leading up to Easter sometimes incited Christians to murderous rages against Jews because of their strong theme of Jewish deicide. And for many centuries, Passover/Easter time was when the blood libel occurred. The blood libel was the belief that Jews used the blood of young Christians to make matzah (unleavened bread) to celebrate Passover. As ludicrous as this claim may seem, it was often put forward by Christian authorities, leading to rioting and even pogroms (mass destruction and murder directed against the Jewish community).

It is against this uncomfortable and even horrific back-drop that the recent emergence of so many Christian churches celebrating Passover with seders seems all the more remarkable. In our own experience, not a year goes by that a church does not invite one of us to lead a Passover seder. Although some Jews may be uncomfortable with Christians embracing the holiday of Passover, we believe that if a church respectfully holds a seder as a way of understanding Judaism, and thus understanding the roots of Christianity, it should be encouraged to do so. From a Jewish perspective, there is some fear that a church may try to Christianize the elements of the seder to make it fit within the Easter narrative. As long as this boundary is not crossed, a church seder performed out of respect and a real desire to learn makes for another small *tikkun,* "repair," in Christian-Jewish relations.

8

SHAVUOT

REMEMBERING THE
GIVING OF THE TORAH

> Count off seven weeks; from the time the sickle is first
> put to the standing corn, you should begin to number
> seven weeks. Then you should observe the feast of
> weeks to Adonai your God after the measure of the
> freewill-offering of your hand, which you should give,
> according to the manner in which Adonai your God has
> blessed you.
>
> —DEUTERONOMY 16:9–10

Bleary-eyed. Bleary-eyed and exhausted. Bleary-eyed,
exhausted, and giddy. These are not the usual words to describe
a Jewish holiday, but the observance of Shavuot is no ordinary
observance. On Shavuot the Jewish people commemorate the
giving of the Torah at Mount Sinai. There is a story that the
Jews were caught sleeping when God came down on Mount
Sinai to deliver the Torah; to ensure that this does not happen
again, we stay up all night studying Torah. Thus, this makes
Shavuot a holiday of sleep deprivation as well as one filled with
great excitement.

Like Passover and Sukkot, Shavuot is connected to the
agricultural cycle and also has meaning that transcends nature.
Unlike Passover and Sukkot, Shavuot is only a two-day holiday. But it is the only holiday that we anticipate by actually
counting the days until we reach its celebration. This period of

counting, which is connected to the spring harvest, begins with the second night of Passover and is called the *Omer.* The counting of the *Omer* lasts for forty-nine days and culminates with the celebration of *Shavuot.*

THE BASICS: SHAVUOT AND SPIRITUAL REDEMPTION

Shavuot is observed on the sixth and seventh day of the Hebrew month of Sivan, generally in early June. In Israel and by members of the Reform movement, it is observed for one day. The rest of the Jewish world celebrates Shavuot for two days. While Passover and Sukkot may celebrate a physical emancipation, Shavuot acknowledges more of a spiritual redemption. As a result, there are no ritual objects uniquely associated with this holiday. For most people, the major require-ment may be a lengthy nap before the holiday begins, since many communities sponsor an all-night study session called a *tikkun layl Shavuot.* This tradition originated in the Zohar (the central work of Jewish mysticism), in which it is stated that those who stay awake all night in anticipation of receiving the Torah are to be praised. The mystics believed that the heavens opened at midnight and favorably received the thoughts, study, and prayers of those who had remained awake. The entire night of study was likened to the hours of preparation prior to a wed-ding. The Moroccan Jewish community believed that staying up all night guaranteed you life for the next year.

HISTORICAL BACKGROUND

Shavuot began as a springtime harvest festival that celebrated the first fruits of the season. The first wheat ripened approximately fifty days after the first barley. This first barley was brought to the ancient Temple one day after Passover began. Over time, Shavuot became more of a celebration of God's revelation than a harvest festival.

In Exodus 23:16, Shavuot is called the Feast of the Harvest, since the holiday falls during the wheat harvest season. It was from this wheat that two loaves of bread were baked and brought to the ancient Temple as an offering, after which the new season's wheat could be used for the offerings of grain. These grains—referred to as *meal offerings*—were used in the ancient Temple in much the same way as were animal sacrifices. However, in the case of harvest festivals, such as Shavuot, the grain that was harvested was offered. As part of the offering, some of it was shared with the priests in the Temple for their own nourishment.

In Deuteronomy 16:9–10, we are told to "count off seven weeks ... then you should observe the feast of weeks to Adonai your God." Once the Temple was destroyed and the people were exiled from the Land of Israel, with the agricultural context for the holiday lost, the Rabbis (in the second century CE) were fearful that the observance of Shavuot would decline, and therefore they determined that the giving of the Torah coincided with Shavuot.

Because of its connection to Passover and the fact that little ritual was prescribed for Shavuot, it is possible that it did not have independent holiday status and was instead simply the capping of a holiday season that began with Passover. This is not unlike the fall holidays, which form a network of special times associated with the period of intense introspection that begins a month before Rosh Hashanah and concludes with the end of Sukkot/Simchat Torah.

SHAVUOT CUSTOMS AND OBSERVANCES

It is customary to eat dairy foods (rather than meat) on Shavuot. This tradition is derived from many sources, including the text from the Song of Songs that suggests that "the knowledge of Torah is like milk and honey under the tongue" (4:11). Another reason given for this custom is that since the dietary laws were not yet established at the time Shavuot originated, the Jewish people chose not to risk the possibility of any errors in eating. Another food custom for this holiday is the baking or purchase of longer-than-usual challah breads, symbolic of the offering required of Jews to bring to the ancient Temple. Many longstanding Jewish communities have their own food specialty associated with Shavuot. In some Sephardic communities, for example, seven-layer cakes are popular on Shavuot. Mystics believe that there are seven spheres that separate humans from God. Thus, the seven layers of the cake represent the mystical seven celestial spheres that God had to traverse to deliver the Torah to the Jewish people. The cake is often decorated with various symbols relevant to the journey of the Jewish people.

As with nearly all Jewish holidays, the festival of Shavuot is introduced with the lighting of candles and a traditional blessing over wine called the *Kiddush*. Additionally, a prayer of thanksgiving, familiar to many holidays and other occasions, is recited. Here are the blessings recited at the Shavuot service:

Candlelighting

Barukh atah Adonai Eloheinu Melekh ha'olam asher kid'shanu b'mitzvotav v'tzivanu l'hadlik ner shel Yom Tov.

Praised are You, Adonai our God, Sovereign of the
universe, who made us holy by *mitzvot*
[commandments] and instructed us to light the
holiday candles.

Over Wine

Barukh atah Adonai Eloheinu Melekh ha'olam, borei p'ri hagafen.
Barukh atah Adonai Eloheinu Melekh ha'olam, asher bachar
banu mikol am v'rom'manu mikol lashon v'kid'shanu
b'mitzvotav vatiten lanu Adonai Eloheinu b'ahavah mo'adim
l'simchah chagim uz'manim l'sasson et yom chag haShavuot
hazeh, z'man matan torateinu mikra kodesh zeikher litzi'at
Mitzrayim.
Ki vanu vacharta v'otanu kidashta mikol ha'amim umo'adei
kodsh'kha b'simcha uv'sasson hinchaltanu.
Barukh atah Adonai, m'kadesh Yisra'eil v'haz'manim.
Praised are You, Adonai our God, Sovereign of the
universe, who creates fruit of the vine.
Praised are You, Adonai our God, Sovereign of the
universe, who has chosen and distinguished us from
all others by adding holiness to our lives with *mitzvot*
[commandments].
Lovingly have You given us festivals for joy and holidays
for happiness, among them this day of Shavuot, season of
the giving of the Torah, a day of sacred assembly recalling
the Exodus from Egypt.
Thus You have chosen us, endowing us with holiness
from among all peoples by granting us Your hallowed
festivals in happiness and joy.
Praised are You, God, who hallows the people Israel
and the festivals.

A Prayer of Thanksgiving

*Barukh atah Adonai Eloheinu Melekh ha'olam shehecheyanu
v'kiymanu v'higi'anu laz'man hazeh.*
Praised are You, Adonai our God, Sovereign of the
universe, who has given us life, sustained us, and helped
us reach this moment.

Other Shavuot Rituals

In some European communities, it was customary to initiate
children in the study of Torah on Shavuot. Often, as children
learned the letters of the Hebrew alphabet, teachers would give
children honey, symbolizing the sweetness of Torah study.
Today, religious schools often give students their own Bibles on
Shavuot. Many Hebrew high schools hold confirmation exer-
cises during one of the Shavuot services, a practice initiated by
the Reform movement, initially borrowed from Protestant
Christianity.

Some synagogues adorn their pulpits with flowers, leaves,
and plants on Shavuot. Others place intricate flower paper cut-
tings on the windows and scatter spices and rose petals
throughout. The synagogue is decorated for many reasons,
including to portray the themes of springtime and renewal.
While there are various explanations for this custom, we pre-
fer the legend that the foot of Mount Sinai (where the Jews
stood in awe, awaiting the granting of the Torah) suddenly
flowered in anticipation of the Torah, becoming carpeted with
greens and sweet-smelling flowers.

In the Jewish communities of some Arab countries,
people would ascend to the roof of the synagogue on Shavuot
and throw apples down to the ground. This custom is meant
to symbolize the similarity of the Israelites at Mount Sinai to
the growth of an apple. The fruit of the apple begins to

develop before the leaf. In the same way, Israelites proclaimed "We will do and we will listen," before they could listen to the commandments and analyze them, contrary to what might be expected as the logical order of behavior: "We will first listen and then we will act."

Another custom at Shavuot is the reading of the book of Ruth. Ruth famously decides to become a part of the Jewish people after the death of her Jewish husband. She tells her Jewish mother-in-law Naomi, "Wherever you go, I will go; wherever you lodge, I will lodge; your people will be my people; your God, my God. Where you die, I will die, and there I will be buried" (Ruth 1:16–17). Just as Shavuot represents the acceptance of the Torah by the Jewish people, Ruth "accepts" the Torah through her conversion to Judaism. Perhaps inspired by Ruth's choice to cast her lot with the Jewish people, those studying for conversion to Judaism often choose to complete their learning, go to the *mikvah* (ritual bath), and enter the covenant before Shavuot. Some women choose to take the name Ruth for their Hebrew name. In many places, these Jews-by-choice (as converts are often called) are called to the Torah for the first time on Shavuot.

There is a special Shavuot insert added to the core prayer (the *Amidah,* known as the standing prayer, since it is said while standing) in the morning and evening services called *Ya'aleh V'yavoh,* as well as in the grace after meals. Both are found in most Jewish prayer books. The *Hallel* Psalms (Psalms 113–118) are also read during the morning service for Shavuot.

The public reading of the Torah on Shavuot includes the recitation of the Ten Commandments; the entire congregation stands, as part of the reenactment of the receiving of the Torah (Exodus 19–20). On the second day, the origin of the holiday as a harvest festival is acknowledged in Deuteronomy 15:19–16:17. A portion from the book of Numbers that specifies the relevant sacrifices is read on both days (28:26–31). A selection from the first chapter of Ezekiel is read as the reading from Prophets for the first day. During Ezekiel's participation in the captivity of the Jewish people in Babylon, he receives a vision of the creatures of heaven adoring God. On the second day, a selection from Habakkuk is read (chapter 3) in which the prophet recalls the historic revelation of God during the Exodus.

Sephardic Jews read a *ketubah* (wedding contract) following the opening of the ark on Shavuot morning. This marital agreement establishes God as the groom and the Jewish people as the bride.

On the second day of the festival, the *Yizkor* (Memorial) service is recited. The *Yizkor* service is intended to honor the memory of loved ones who have died. At holiday time, as families gather, we are particularly sensitive to the loss we feel for those who are no longer with us. This is a common concluding feature for a number of the holidays including Yom Kippur and Passover.

The Counting of the Omer

The forty-nine-day period that starts from the second night of Passover and continues until Shavuot is called *sefirat ha-omer,* "the counting of the *Omer.*" The tradition is to say a blessing for each day of the counting during evening prayers. Jewish law prescribes that if we forget to say the counting blessing even one evening, we may count, without saying the blessing, during daylight hours the following morning or afternoon, then resume the regular counting with the blessing that evening. If, however, we forget to enumerate the *Omer* for one or more full days, subsequent counting is performed without the recitation of the blessing for the remainder of that year's period of the *Omer.*

By the Middle Ages, the period of the counting of the *Omer* was associated with mourning. There is a story from the Talmud about the death of thousands of students of a famous rabbi from a plague during this time of year. As a result of this association with mourning, weddings traditionally do not take place during this period, and men do not get haircuts.

On the thirty-third day of the counting of the *Omer,* a minor holiday known as Lag B'Omer is marked. This day provides a break in the forty-nine-day period: Marriages can take place, and men can cut their hair. In contemporary Israel, Lag B'Omer is observed by lighting bonfires and having picnics.

OTHER SHAVUOT TEXTS

An eleventh-century poem called *Akdamut* is traditionally read during the morning service on the first day of Shavuot. It emphasizes the loyalty of the Jewish people to the Torah and the love that God expresses for the People of Israel.

Liturgical poems that feature fanciful accounts of revelation are woven into the liturgy, and rhymed verses of the 613 commandments, called *Azharot,* are read. Psalm 68 serves as an anthem of sorts for the festival. This psalm focuses on the Exodus, the revelation at Sinai, and God's providence. It serves a second purpose, since it describes the mountain of revelation as one of many peaks (verse 15), which can be punned in Hebrew as a mountain of many cheeses, another possible reason for the tradition of eating cheese-filled foods.

CHRISTIAN PARALLELS TO SHAVUOT

Pentecost (from the Greek for "fiftieth") is a festival observed on the seventh Sunday (fiftieth day) after Easter. This commemorates the descent of the Holy Spirit on the Apostles as they celebrated Shavuot, according to Acts 2:1–4. It was a time for the administration of the sacrament of baptism in the early church. The Pentecost festival is called Whitsunday or Whitsun in the Church of England and other Anglican churches, an allusion to the white robes traditionally worn by the newly baptized. This day is particularly striking because of the extensive adornment of flowers in the church. (That may be why some rabbis prohibited the extensive decorating of the synagogue with plants and flowers on Shavuot.)

9

TISHA B'AV AND OTHER
SPECIAL DAYS

Why do You forget us forever; why do You so long forsake us? Turn us to You, Adonai, and we shall be turned;
renew our days as of old.

—LAMENTATIONS 5:20–21

SADNESS AND MOURNING

Tisha B'Av is considered the saddest day in the Jewish calendar. If you enter a synagogue on this day, you may see people
with a solemn expression on their faces, sitting unshaven on
low stools and chanting mournful dirges. The rituals of
Tisha B'Av are similar to the Jewish rituals for mourning a
loved one who has died, but the entire community mourns on
Tisha B'Av.

Tisha B'Av is literally a date—the ninth of Av. (Av is the
name of the Hebrew month in which this commemoration
takes place. It is usually observed in July or August.) On the
ninth and tenth of Av, in the year 70 CE, the Roman legions
under Titus laid siege to the Temple in Jerusalem. In a bloody
conflict, Roman soldiers killed the Jewish defenders of
Jerusalem, set the Temple on fire, and sent the remaining Jews
of Jerusalem into exile. The taking of Jerusalem by Titus was
the culmination of years of civil war among the Jews and of
Jewish political revolt against the Roman authorities. Some

scholars estimate that the violence in those years of revolt and civil war took over one million Jewish lives.

Tisha B'Av is not only important as a day of mourning for the multitudes of Jews who perished, but perhaps even more so for the effects the destruction of the Temple would have on the course of Jewish history. The Temple was the center of Jewish life. While the Temple stood, sacrifice was the primary mode of worshiping God, and sacrifices were offered three times daily. On the major festivals—Passover, Shavuot, and Sukkot—people made pilgrimages to the Temple. The destruction of the Temple meant not only a loss of life, but potentially the end of the practice of Judaism itself.

RESPONSES TO CATASTROPHE

The destruction of the Temple may have marked a decisive moment for Judaism and for Christianity as well. With the cultic center of Judaism—God's dwelling place on earth, as it was known—destroyed, what was to become of Judaism? Some Jews simply abandoned the faith and assimilated into the majority Hellenist culture. For a small group of Jews, however, the destruction of the Temple was a sign that the old way of Judaism was dead and that a new covenant was being established. Believers in Jesus, who until this time had still been part of the Jewish community, saw in the destruction of the Temple the sign that Jesus was meant to be the new way of life.

For the Jews who remained loyal to Judaism, Jewish hope took two different directions. There were some Jews who were committed to the idea of rebuilding the Temple and regaining political control of Jerusalem. In 132 CE a Jewish leader named Simon Bar Kochba, with the support of many of the Jews who remained in Judea, revolted against the Roman authorities. This revolt ended in his death and in the expulsion of his followers. This would be the last attempt to gain Jewish authority over Jerusalem for almost two thousand years.

With Bar Kochba's defeat, Judaism resigned itself to life in exile. But Jews remained theologically committed to a restoration of Jews in Israel and to a rebuilding of the Temple. As part of the daily liturgy, Jews throughout the diaspora—in France, Poland, Germany, Tunisia, Egypt, wherever Jews found themselves—prayed for a return to Israel and its restoration. The dream of returning to Israel was kept alive for almost two thousand years (from 70 CE to 1948).

While Bar Kochba was plotting revolt against Rome to rebuild the Temple, the other path that faithful Jews took after the Temple's destruction was to reformulate Judaism without the Temple. Rabbi Yohanan Ben Zakkai became the pivotal figure in this endeavor. Ben Zakkai was a leading rabbinic authority who surreptitiously fled Jerusalem by pretending he was dead. He then set up a new center of Jewish learning in Yavneh, a city along the Mediterranean coast, west of Jerusalem. Ben Zakkai transformed Judaism by making every Jew responsible for what was formerly the domain of the priest. In place of three daily sacrifices led by a priest, each Jew was now instructed to pray three times daily. In place of the sacrificial altar, Jews were to consider the table on which they ate an altar. In place of the Temple, the synagogue/study house became the center of Jewish religious life. Most significant, perhaps, was the theological change, the reformulation of who God was, which enabled Judaism to survive the loss of the Temple.

Theological Response to Catastrophe

Although the Romans destroyed the Temple, the Jewish writing of the time indicates that Rome had little to do with the Temple's destruction—apart from actually razing it. The

Roman army was simply a tool utilized by God, who allowed the destruction of the Temple because of the various sins of the Jewish people. This is a stunning and potentially quite disturbing theology, blaming the victims for their suffering—a position rejected by most contemporary liberal thinkers. A well-known story in Jewish tradition as to why the Temple was destroyed suggests that it was a dispute between two Jewish enemies, one of whom is insulted by the other and then incites Rome to crush Jerusalem as a result of his insult (as noted in the Babylonian Talmud, *Gittin* 56b). When the Jewish people experienced anything punitive at the hands of their enemies, they often looked inward, searching for the reason why God might have allowed the situation to occur—or even directed it. In the case of the destruction of the Temple, some of the Rabbis argued that it was the result of senseless hatred (*sinhat hinam*) between Jews, a case of members of the same family fighting each other. God punishes Israel with the destruction of the Temple and the dispersion of the Jews as a result.

The power of this idea is that it accounts for God's apparent impotence during the siege of Jerusalem. If God were all powerful, how could God allow the divine abode to be destroyed? The Rabbis argue that it must have been God's intention all along. Nevertheless, God does not take pleasure in this destruction. God mourns with the people when the Temple is destroyed. The Rabbis in the Midrash even suggest that when the Temple is destroyed, God puts on sackcloth and ashes, walks barefoot, and rends God's divine garments, just as people do when they are mourning (*Lamentations Rabbah* 1:1). God mourns the loss of God's people; God then goes into exile with the People of Israel. It is this theological idea that became crucial for Jewish survival. No longer would God dwell in the Temple in Jerusalem. Instead, God would dwell everywhere. Hence, the Rabbis begin using as the name for God *Ha-Makom,* "The Place," to evoke the notion that God is everyplace and no place in particular. God is to be found wherever people call out to God. In the extraordinary number of places that Jews end up as a result of the dispersion, God goes with them. God's exile with the people is central to Jewish history.

TISHA B'AV CUSTOMS AND OBSERVANCES

With the establishment of the modern State of Israel and a return to Jerusalem, some Jews have called into question the need for marking a day of mourning for Jerusalem. In terms of importance, Tisha B'Av is not as significant as the other holidays presented in this book. Nonetheless, Tisha B'Av remains a day of mourning for observant Jews. Similar to Yom Kippur, it is a full-day fast that actually lasts for twenty-five hours. On Tisha B'Av, the ritually observant Jew does not wash and refrains from sexual relations.

Preparations for Tisha B'Av begin three weeks before the actual day (usually at the beginning of July). The seventeenth of Tammuz—three weeks before the ninth of Av—marks the date when the Romans breached the walls of Jerusalem. Weddings are not performed during this three-week period, and the choice of weekly prophetic readings in the synagogue detail ancient Israel's sinful ways.

On the day of Tisha B'Av, Jews in synagogue sit on hard benches or low stools, a symbol of mourning. Mournful dirges (*kenot* in Hebrew) are sung. The book of Lamentations is also chanted. In some synagogues, Lamentations is chanted by candlelight to enhance the gloomy feeling. Lamentations recounts the destruction of the First Temple and those who survived it in lurid detail. Jerusalem is laid waste; its inhabitants suffer from wretched deprivations. The book of Lamentations ends with the verse "Unless you have utterly rejected us, and are exceed-ingly angry with us" (5:22), but the custom is to chant the next to last verse again as the ending, "Turn us to You, Adonai, and we shall be turned; renew our days as of old" (5:21). It offers an ending note of hope amid all the despair.

The holiday of Tisha B'Av is an acting out of despair. Everything is done to reinforce the sense of gloom and mourning for those who died at the destruction of the Temple and an acknowledgment of all the moments in Jewish history when Jews have been killed. It should be noted that the holi-day that follows Tisha B'Av, just seven weeks later, is Rosh Hashanah, the new year, the chance for a new beginning. Jewish life is marked by an audacious sense of hope, optimism despite life's miseries. The Jewish holiday cycle reflects such optimism. Despite the tragedy of the destruction of the Temple and the loss of life, the saddest day of the Jewish year quickly gives way to one of the most joyous.

CHRISTIAN PARALLELS TO TISHA B'AV

There is no day in the Christian year that offers a direct paral-lel to Tisha B'Av, but there is one surprising correlation. The Christian calendar does not include any significant holidays to remember a particular tragedy in history, but one day does reflect the destruction of the Temple. The closest parallel to Tisha B'Av is Good Friday, the day when Jesus was crucified and died. The death of Jesus remains the most profound expe-rience of destruction for Christians. The suffering that Jews relive on Tisha B'Av is akin to the suffering and death that some Christians see as a core aspect of Christianity.

Further, and most interesting as a parallel to Tisha B'Av, the Gospels utilize Temple imagery in describing Jesus's death.

In John 2:20–22 the Gospel says, "Jesus answered and said to them, 'Destroy this temple and in three days I will raise it up.' They said, 'This temple has been under construction for forty-six years, and you will raise it up in three days?' But he was speaking about the temple of his body. Therefore, when he was raised from the dead, his disciples remembered that he had said this, and they came to believe the scripture and the word Jesus had spoken."

Mark, Matthew, and Luke all include passages that describe the Temple curtain being torn in two when Jesus is crucified. In Luke 23:44–47, the Gospel tells us, "It was now about noon and darkness came over the whole land until three in the afternoon because of an eclipse of the sun. Then the veil of the Temple was torn down the middle. Jesus cried out in a loud voice, 'Father, into your hands I commend my spirit'; and when he had said this he breathed his last. The centurion who witnessed what had happened glorified God and said, 'This man was innocent beyond doubt.'"

For the Gospel writers, Jesus served a similar theological function as the Temple did in Jewish theology. The Temple was the means by which Jews could expiate their sins and draw closer to God. The Temple was the abode of God in this world. These are all theological ideas that Jesus symbolized as well. It is therefore not surprising that Jesus is compared to the Temple.

The analogy should not be taken too far, however. For Christian theology, Jesus's death was a necessary step toward resurrection. Good Friday leads toward the redemptive message of Easter. For Jews, the destruction of the Temple has no such redemptive quality. As a result, Tisha B'Av is a day solely for mourning and reflecting on the past as a way of preparing for the present and the ultimate future.

YOM HASHOAH/
HOLOCAUST REMEMBRANCE DAY

The sound of an air-raid siren blast is heard all over Israel. Cars and buses pull off the road, students stand quietly, shoppers pause, everything, everyone comes to a complete standstill. It is Yom Hashoah in Israel. Yom Hashoah is the day that commemorates the loss of six million Jews in the Holocaust. In Israel the day is observed by ceremonies honoring those who were killed and, for two minutes in the morning, air-raid sirens are sounded throughout the entire country and everyone stops what they are doing to mourn and to remember.

The word for the Nazis' murder of six million Jews in Hebrew is *Shoah* (conflagration by fire), so the name *Yom Hashoah* means "Day of the Holocaust." American Jews often refer to the Holocaust by its Hebrew name, *Shoah,* to distinguish the Jewish genocide from other historical genocides, such as the Armenian genocide of the early twentieth century. The Israeli government determined that Yom Hashoah should be observed on the twenty-seventh of the Hebrew month of Nisan, a few weeks after Passover. The date was chosen because it was near the date when the Warsaw ghetto uprising occurred in 1943, the most significant revolt by Jews against the Nazis. The Warsaw uprising began on the fifteenth of Nisan, but that is the first night of Passover, so the date was pushed back a few weeks. It is worth noting that the Israeli government set the date to coincide with the Warsaw revolt. The government wanted to preserve the memory not only of those who died, but also of those who resisted under such unspeakable conditions.

There is much about the observance of Holocaust Remembrance Day that is still being determined. The Holocaust occurred only sixty years ago, so the customs and liturgy for its remembrance are still fluid and have not yet been standardized. Depending on where the commemoration is held, whether a public event or one that takes place in a synagogue or Jewish Community Center, observances may include the following: lighting six candles in memory of the six million Jews who perished; reading a partial list of those who were killed; listening to survivors speak about their experiences; honoring righteous gentiles who saved the lives of Jews; and reading poetry or words related to the Holocaust. In some synagogues the regular prayers are recited with certain psalms and prayers of mourning added to the service, and in some synagogues there is no regular liturgy at all, simply poems or recollections.

Many alternative ways of observing the day have also been developed in the past few years. Some people have written dramatic scrolls that tell the story of the Holocaust following the form of the biblical book of Lamentations. Some propose that Yom HaShoah be a fast day like Tisha B'Av; others have suggested the day be one of complete silence to reflect how inadequate words are in light of the immense horror. The many different ways that the day is observed reflect the different ways the Holocaust itself is understood. Rabbi Joseph Soleveitchik, the leading Orthodox rabbi in America for decades, thought that the day should be observed as part of Tisha B'Av. Doing so places the Holocaust in a religious context, connecting it with other great tragedies that have befallen Jews. But other modern thinkers, such as Rabbi Irving "Yitz" Greenberg, see the Holocaust as a unique event in Jewish history, which utterly transforms the covenant the Jewish people have with God.

Rabbi Greenberg notes that the Holocaust has shattered the idea of a covenant that God enjoins on the People of Israel. The covenant has always been one of the central tenets of Jewish thought, and Rabbi Greenberg says that as a result of the devastation of the Holocaust, Jews can no longer perceive of God as an equal partner in this covenant. The Jewish people themselves have become the "senior partners" in this covenant, and we make a choice to keep faith with a God who was absent at the moment of the Jewish people's greatest crisis. Yom Hashoah should be a day that reflects our commitment to God, but it must also reflect this new covenant that has arisen out of the ashes of Auschwitz. He believes that unique rituals like a Holocaust scroll are necessary to establish this idea.

If *Jewish Holidays* were written in another fifty years or so, the exact meaning of Holocaust Remembrance Day would probably be clearer. But we are still living very much in the aftermath of the greatest tragedy the Jewish people have ever known; there is much concern about whether the Holocaust will be remembered at all in the future. Even as the importance of the Holocaust becomes more fixed in the minds of Americans by the establishment of the Holocaust Museum in Washington, D.C., and the viewing by millions of Steven Spielberg's film *Schindler's List,* the number of living survivors who can bear personal witness to what happened are dwindling. The one aspect of remembering the Holocaust that everyone can agree on is that there is a need to remember. "Never Forget" has become a communal rallying cry for secular and religious Jews alike.

Yom Hazikaron/Day of Remembrance and Yom Ha'atzmaut/ Israeli Independence Day

One week after the siren of Yom Hashoah, another siren is sounded throughout Israel. Again, everything comes to a standstill. One week after Holocaust Remembrance Day is Yom Hazikaron—the day to remember soldiers who have fallen defending the State of Israel. This day is observed primarily in Israel because the holiday is so connected with Israeli identity. Like Yom Hashoah, Yom Hazikaron is observed by memorial services, and many families go to the graves of relatives who died in Israel's wars. Many high schools hold observances, with pictures and memorials to students from the school who have died in Israeli wars.

Theodor Herzl, the founder of the modern Zionist movement, said that "if you will it, it is no dream." Israel's existence was a two-thousand-year-old dream that became a reality. From a religious perspective, the founding of Israel was the ingathering of the exiles, the promise made to the Jewish people by God that they would one day return to the Promised Land. Many Jews do not see modern Israel in such starkly religious terms but understand it as a dream fulfilled nonetheless. After thousands of years of persecution and marginalization, the Jewish people have security through a homeland. Like Yom Hashoah, the day is thus observed by both religious and secular Jews. Israel is a unique melding of peoplehood and religion, and Yom Hazikaron has importance from a religious and a cultural context.

Just after sundown on Yom Hazikaron, Israelis transform their mourning into the celebration of Yom Ha'atzmaut, Israeli Independence Day. It is observed on the fifth of the Hebrew month of Iyar, marking May 14, 1948, when Israel declared its independence. For many years this was observed in Israel by military parades, but more recently Israelis have been observing the day by holding family picnics and other family festivities. In the synagogue Yom Ha'atzmaut is celebrated with the singing of *Hallel* Psalms (Psalms 113–118) of thanksgiving. American synagogues often present an Israeli cultural program—a speaker, a film, or a program or presentation of Israeli dancing—as a way of celebrating Israel on Yom Ha'atzmaut.

TU B'SHEVAT

Long before there was Earth Day, there was Tu B'Shevat, a not so well-known Jewish holiday that celebrates trees. Tu B'Shevat, like Tisha B'Av, is a date on the Jewish calendar, the fifteenth of the month of Shevat, usually occurring in late January or early February. The holiday traces its roots back to the time of the Mishnah (the first code of Jewish law, compiled in 200 CE). In a section of the Mishnah called *Rosh Hashanah,* the Rabbis tell us that there are four new years: a new year for kings and festivals; a new year for tithes for cattle; a new year for years (Rosh Hashanah); and a new year for the trees. The idea of different "new years" should not surprise us, since we observe a fiscal new year, a school new year, and the like. The four different new years mentioned in the Mishnah similarly represent different economic and social seasons. The new year for the trees is an economic marker. The fruit of trees that blossom before the fifteenth of Shevat are tithed before the end of the year, and the fruit of trees that blossom after the fifteenth of Shevat in the following year (Babylonian Talmud, *Rosh Hashanah* 15b). Tithes were gifts given to the priests in the ancient Temple in Jerusalem. The particular date of the fifteenth of Shevat was chosen because most of the annual rain in Israel has fallen by this date (as noted in the Babylonian Talmud, *Rosh Hashanah* 13a).

With the destruction of the Temple and the end of tithing, Tu B'Shevat evolved from tax day into a celebration of nature. This was primarily due to a highly influential group of Jewish mystics who lived in Safed—in the Land of Israel—

in the sixteenth century. They created a Tu B'Shevat seder, modeled on the Passover seder. Participants read selections from the Torah and Rabbinic literature and ate seven types of fruits and nuts that are mentioned in the Bible. According to Deuteronomy 8:8, Israel is a "land of wheat and barley, of vines, figs and pomegranates, a land of olive trees, and [date] honey." Participants in the seder also drank four cups of wine, just as we do at a Passover seder. However, at a Tu B'Shevat seder, participants drink cups of wine with varying colors: white wine (to symbolize winter); white with some red (a harbinger of the coming of spring); red with some white (early spring); and finally all red (spring and summer).

The mystical Tu B'Shevat seder remained an interesting but relatively unobserved Jewish ritual until the recent burgeoning of the environmental movement and a renaissance of interest in Jewish mysticism. Many synagogues have begun holding Tu B'Shevat seders modeled on the mystical seder. These seders draw upon the rich history of Jewish environmentalism and care of the trees for inspiration. The Torah states, "When you lay siege to a city for a long time, fighting against it to capture it, do not destroy its trees by putting an ax to them, because you can eat their fruit. Do not cut them down. Are the trees of the field people, that you should besiege them?" (Deuteronomy 20:19). The Torah itself is likened to a tree in a prayer said every time the Torah is read in public, "[The Torah] is a tree of life to all who hold fast to it" (Proverbs 3:18).

The celebration of Tu B'Shevat is also a time for tree planting. The Jewish National Fund, a well-known organization that develops forests in Israel, has made the day a special day for planting trees in Israel. Some Jewish communities urge their members on Tu B'Shevat to give charity to the Jewish National Fund as a way of observing the holiday.

10

SHABBAT
OBSERVING THE SABBATH

Remember the Sabbath to sanctify it.

—EXODUS 20:8

Keep the Sabbath day to guard it.

—DEUTERONOMY 5:12

THE BASICS

Maybe it is middle age, but I, Kerry, can actually feel my body beginning to shut down as I make my way home each Friday afternoon in anticipation of Shabbat (the Sabbath). I can push all week long—early mornings and late nights—but, come Friday, I am ready to completely unwind. It isn't just the bodily rest that I crave; it is the deep spiritual nourishment that the Sabbath provides. By separating myself from the frenzy of the world that surrounds me all week long, I can focus on the needs of my soul throughout Shabbat. It is an island away from secular intrusions on my spiritual world.

Shabbat is unlike any other day. For starters, it is twenty-five hours long. It begins on Friday afternoon eighteen minutes before sunset and goes through Saturday night after the stars have come out. Because the start of Shabbat changes each week with the changing time of sunset, I am forced to admit that I am not in control of the world around me. So I consciously let go and let God lead the way to holiness for me.

The Sabbath begins with the lighting of candles and the short blessing marking the time as sacred and special. This is followed by a *Kiddush* prayer (over wine or grape juice) to sanctify the day, the blessing of children and spouse, a festive meal with singing, and *Birkat Hamazon,* a prayer of thanksgiving or "Grace after Meals," as it is sometimes called. The basic elements are repeated, in a modified form, at Shabbat lunch on Saturday and at a third meal (known by its Hebrew translation, *seudah shelishit*) that takes place in the late afternoon or early evening depending on the time of year, as well as with worship and study along the way. The Sabbath concludes with a ritual called *Havdalah,* as explained later in this chapter.

The primary goal in observing the Sabbath is to limit the intrusion of the workaday world so that we can focus on the more important issue of spiritual renewal. The Rabbis (that is, the Rabbis of ancient times—with a capital *R*) established prohibited labors on the Sabbath as a guide. They deduced these prohibited activities from the various tasks that were required to build the ancient Tabernacle. In this way, they transformed the idea of building sacred space into building sacred time.

BROAD STROKES OF SABBATH OBSERVANCE

I, Dan, keep two kinds of Sabbaths, as distinguished by my friend Rachel and my ultra-Orthodox cousins. They both observe the Sabbath, but they do so in different ways. My cousins in Williamsburg, Brooklyn, observe the Sabbath by following a vast array of rules as to what they can and cannot do. They spend all Friday cooking and cleaning, readying themselves for the Sabbath when they will not use electricity, the television, or the computer, and they will not spend any money. Rachel observes the Sabbath as well. She wakes up on Saturday morning and goes to the gym to work out. When she gets home, she spends time with her husband and then heads to her favorite bookstore, where they have wide comfortable chairs, good coffee, and don't mind people spending a few hours reading. She believes that the Sabbath is about giving oneself joy in life, and few things bring her as much pleasure as an afternoon browsing through books.

My cousins in Williamsburg would never acknowledge that Rachel was observing the Sabbath by working out and going shopping at the bookstore. On the other hand, Rachel would hardly equate her Sabbath ritual with my cousins' extensive Sabbath preparations. But the Jewish observance of the Sabbath runs the gamut from my cousins' all-encompassing Shabbat to Rachel's jogging and caffe latte.

For my cousins, the observance of the Sabbath is anchored in traditional Jewish law. The laws concerning Shabbat were laid out in the Mishnah. The Rabbis of the Mishnah tried to define what constitutes "work." In various places in the Bible, we are told that we should observe the Sabbath as rest because God rested on the seventh day after creating the world. But the Bible does not detail precisely what "rest" or "work" encompasses. The Bible does tell us about the poor laborer who was caught gathering wood on the Sabbath and summarily stoned for working on the holy day. But besides gathering wood and lighting a fire, we are given no further information about what constitutes work. The Rabbis of the Mishnah thus attempt to spell out "work." They take their lead from the work that was required to build the Tabernacle that the Israelites brought with them during

117

their desert journey from Egypt to Canaan, and deduce thirty-nine categories of work, what they call *melakha*. While we might not consider them part of our daily work, these categories include planting, tearing, putting two letters together, building, and mixing. Most of the activities on the list are agricultural tasks that reflect the farming society in which the Rabbis lived.

The traditional Sabbath my cousins observe is rather stringent. Following the categories of prohibited work (and later work-related activities that were added to the list), you are not permitted to drive or carry anything outside of your own private space—that means the home (although the Rabbis allowed for private space to be expanded artificially by stringing a wire called an *eruv* around the area—similar to the way power lines are strung—to expand the area in which an individual could carry objects outside the home). You are not permitted to use the phone, to go online, to watch movies, or to shop. You cannot cook, write a letter, or garden. While the list seems overwhelming, the goal is simply to ensure that you separate yourself from any activity that could potentially be work or lead you to work. Thus, you can't even touch certain items, even if you have no intention of using them.

They may appear burdensome, but these restrictions are merely an attempt to help create holy space, by keeping you from the ordinary, the everyday, and elevating you to a more sacred and spiritual plane. By limiting what you are permitted to do, traditional Shabbat restrictions force you to give up the illusion of "control" over your life. Instead, you strip down to life's essentials by getting together with others to eat and talk and celebrate just being alive. If you can't rush off to the shopping mall or work just a little bit more, you can create sacred space in your life to linger over conversation, or to be intimate—physically and spiritually—with your partner. You are able to enter into what Rabbi Abraham Joshua Heschel, considered one of the great rabbis of the twentieth century, calls a "sanctuary of time." This is a period in which you stop trying to change the world (an important part of Jewish ethical life) and simply strive to be in harmony with it.

Unlike my cousins, Rachel does not believe that such strict rules are necessary to experience the Sabbath. For her, observing the Sabbath is much simpler. The Rabbis must have anticipated her attitude when they wrote, in a well-known midrash (a rabbinic legend that explains passages in the Bible), "Shabbat was given only for pleasure." For Rachel, the Sabbath is about doing things that bring her pleasure: working out, reading, drinking coffee. She believes that as long as she is mindful that the activities she is doing are connected to Shabbat, then she is indeed observing the Sabbath.

My cousins and my friend represent two opposing ends of the Shabbat observance spectrum. Rachel sees the Sabbath as being primarily about bringing joy to your life without any specific rules or regulations; my cousins, by contrast, see the Sabbath as a way to set apart one day of the week for complete rest from the world, which, to them, can be accomplished only by following a specific set of guidelines.

Since most of us live somewhere in between, both seem right to me. I try to keep both of these Sabbaths at once. I try to do things that bring me joy while simultaneously recognizing that withdrawing myself from daily activities frees me to experience inner peace in a profound way. Practically, I observe two primary rules to separate myself during Shabbat from my regular days. First, I do not spend any money. This keeps me away from movies, shopping malls, and restaurants. Second, I do not turn on my computer, which keeps me from the temptation to check e-mail, pay a bill online, or finish up that essay or lesson I am preparing.

Franz Rosenzweig, the great Jewish philosopher, said, "The Sabbath is a world revolution." It may seem odd to call the Sabbath revolutionary, since nothing seems less "revolutionary" than a three-thousand-year-old idea. But even if the observance of the Sabbath in our time is not revolutionary, it is, indeed, subversive. There is something subversive about consciously withdrawing from worldly preoccupations. While much of our culture is engaged with commerce, Shabbat is an opportunity to choose not to take part in that world—even if that means just spending Shabbat evening drinking wine with the one you love, reading *Harry Potter* with your child, or being still by yourself and enjoying the solitude.

For some people, it is almost incomprehensible to spend Friday night or Saturday not going out or working. Occasionally, when I see a listing for a concert or a show, or I am invited to a friend's party on a Friday night, I momentarily regret my decision not to participate in these activities on the Sabbath. But, for me, the spiritual discipline of not spending money and not socializing in ways not related to the Sabbath provides me with benefits that transcend the transient joy of a party or a movie. In consistently observing the Sabbath, you can feel an "intuition of eternity," as Heschel calls it. For me, this is not about a magical or mystical experience. Rather, this feeling of Shabbat—set apart from the other days—suffuses me with a profound appreciation for slowing down, for resting, and for appreciating the blessing of time itself.

CREATING THE ISLAND OF SHABBAT

To create space in your life to observe the Sabbath—that island of peace—you have to have some sense of boundaries. It can be hard to create that island, especially if you are very busy all week long. A friend told me, Dan, that the sole rule of Shabbat that she and her family observe is to have Friday night dinner together, the only meal of the week when they are together. At dinner, they go around the table and describe their week—the difficulties they had, and the blessings they felt. Sometimes it is a wonderful experience from the moment they all sit down together; sometimes her teenage daughter opens up in a way she never does during the rest of the week.

But on other occasions her husband will call and say he is going to be late, and her daughter will grumble as she sits down, in that pouty-teenager sort of way, about having to make blessings and share time with her parents. Sometimes the strain of getting together makes everyone mad at each other right through the blessings and into the salad. And if the point of the Sabbath is relaxation, Shabbat appears to be "backfiring." But, she says, eventually, sometime between the main course and dessert, when everyone has decompressed long enough to realize that the goal is to be together just this one time a week, they relax, and the transcendent experience of Shabbat sets in.

THE SABBATH AS A SYMBOL OF ONENESS

The Ten Commandments appear twice in the Hebrew Scriptures. Their revelation at Mount Sinai is first recorded in Exodus and then retold in Deuteronomy. The Book of Exodus says that you should "remember" the Sabbath and keep it holy (Exodus 20:8). Deuteronomy tells us to "guard" the Sabbath (Deuteronomy 5:12). To Jewish readers of the Bible, this slight semantic difference looms large. Commentators see in this shift of wording two ways of observing the Sabbath. "Guarding" Shabbat means adhering to the myriad restrictions imposed by Jewish law that ensure that you will not work. This represents the passive aspect of Shabbat—refraining from work. "Remembering" Shabbat, by contrast, means taking positive actions to increase the joy and peacefulness in your life.

Jewish tradition commemorates the two times the Ten Commandments appear in the Bible by lighting two candles on the Sabbath. This is just one of a number of rituals on Shabbat, which, like the animals on Noah's ark, come in pairs. "Everything pertaining to Shabbat is double...." (*Midrash Tehillim* on 92:1). Customarily, two loaves of challah (braided egg bread) are used to represent the double portion of manna that fell on Friday for the Israelites to gather when they were wandering in the wilderness for forty years. We even have two souls on the Sabbath: The Talmud says that on Shabbat we receive a second soul, which goes away at the conclusion of Shabbat (*Betzah* 16a). The Talmud also says that a pair of angels escort a person home from the synagogue on the eve of the Sabbath (*Shabbat* 119b).

Yet for all the doubling, Shabbat is ultimately about two becoming one. For the mystics it was the male and female aspects of the Divine uniting. The Zohar, the primary text of Kabbalah (the practice of Jewish mysticism), says that just as the male and female aspects of the Divine unite above, so they also unite below in the mystery of the Oneness. Some take this to mean that we should engage in the "double mitzvah" of Shabbat—that is, to make love with our partner, the ultimate expression of two becoming one. The Rabbis even say that the two times where the Ten Commandments appear in the Bible, God actually spoke them at the exact same time, somehow, in the mystery that is the Oneness of God. The Sabbath prayer song *Lekhah Dodi* (Come, My Beloved) says this quite simply: *Shamor vezakhor bediboor echad,* God uttered the words *guard* and *remember* as one word.

Sabbath Candlelighting Customs

As mentioned earlier in this chapter, two candles are usually lit for the Sabbath. They represent the two times the command-ment to observe the Sabbath is given in the Bible, and, specif-ically, the two different words, *shamor* (guard) and *zakhor* (remember) that begin the commandment. But explanations for this custom abound, and some families go beyond this two-candle minimum. Some add a candle for each child. Others use a third candle to represent all their children. Because of the sig-nificance of the number seven in Judaism (for example, the seven days of creation), other customs include the lighting of seven Sabbath candles.

One classic Jewish image is a woman lighting two Sabbath candles before the sun sets. She closes her eyes intently and circles her hands in the air, as if to draw the energy of the candles into her, and she recites the traditional blessing.

The commandment to light candles is meant for men as well as women, but the custom evolved for women to light the candles because they are more closely associated with the home. In liberal Jewish circles, men sometimes light Sabbath candles, yet the custom of women lighting candles still holds sway, even in Jewish communities where women are rabbis and lay Jewish leaders.

After the candles are lit, the blessing is said over the Sabbath candles with eyes closed. Customarily, the person light-ing candles adds a silent blessing for the family. Why are the eyes closed? The answer is not so simple. My mother used to say that no custom in Judaism is ever "so simple." Jews usually say a blessing before performing an act; for example, you say the blessing over bread *before* eating bread. But the blessing over the candles marks the beginning of the Sabbath, and on the Sabbath it is forbidden to create light. So you would be violating the rules of Shabbat by saying the blessing and then lighting the candles. Yet, in this case, you need to say the blessing before the act is done. So it became the custom to light the candles with the eyes closed so you wouldn't see the light while reciting the blessing. When you lower your hands from your eyes, it is as if you had said the blessing before the candles were lit.

Tradition prescribes that you light candles eighteen minutes before sunset. The Sabbath commences officially at sunset, but the lighting of candles marks the beginning of the Sabbath for those who lit the candles. The candlelighting is done early, both to provide a cushion of time so you won't accidentally light candles after sunset, and because it is difficult to determine exactly when sunset occurs.

Sabbath light is the symbol of joy and harmony. We are drawing this joy and harmony into ourselves and our home. The Sabbath is also imagined as a bride and the waving of the hands ushers the bride into the house.

The book of Proverbs says, "The soul of a person is the light of God." After the candles are lit, many people take a moment to reflect on the soul, our inner being, who we are in the world, and how our inner light is connected to God's divine light.

OTHER SHABBAT RITUALS

Here is a very brief sketch of the rituals associated with each time period of Shabbat.

Friday Night Dinner/Friday Night

The Talmud says that a person is accompanied home on Friday night by two angels who guard the way (*Shabbat* 119b). Traditionally, families light Shabbat candles, and then the men go to synagogue for a brief prayer service called *kabbalat Shabbat* (welcoming the Sabbath). They come home and the Shabbat evening ritual begins with the *Kiddush* (a blessing, said over wine, that sanctifies the day) and the *motzi* blessing over challah bread. This is followed by a Sabbath meal.

Sabbath Day

Shabbat morning is traditionally a time when people go to the synagogue. The highlight of the service is the reading of the Torah (the first five books of the Bible) portion of the week, which is designed to help us reexperience the revelation at Sinai. It was at Sinai that the ancient Israelites entered into a covenantal relationship with God on their way through the desert. Sinai became the turning point for the Israelites and marked their move from a slave people to a free nation. We go to the synagogue to pray, to be with friends, and to celebrate the joys of Jewish community.

Saturday Sunset: Havdalah

Just as the Sabbath is ushered in with a ritual act of candlelighting, so we leave the Sabbath with a similar ritual act that involves light. It is a bittersweet time. It is also a time steeped in mystery as the daylight slips into darkness. We hate to let go of the Sabbath. This brief ritual marks the end of the Sabbath and helps us to make the transition back into the workaday world—even though most of us don't work on Saturday night or Sunday. The *Havdalah* ritual takes place at sundown, some twenty-five hours after lighting Sabbath candles. This lovely, simple ceremony includes wine, a special braided candle, and fragrant spices. The ceremony is a sensuous experience of enchanting lights and sweet-smelling aromas.

The *Havdalah* ceremony begins with a song that invites the prophet Elijah—who will herald the coming of the Messiah, according to Jewish tradition—into our midst. It continues with a paragraph taken from the Psalms that speaks of God as the source of redemption, followed by four brief blessings. The first blessing is said over wine. The second one is recited over spices—a reminder of the sweet fragrance of the Sabbath and a way to revive the soul, which has been diminished as a result of the Sabbath's departure. Then comes a blessing said over the multiwicked *Havdalah* candle that acknowledges the creator of the flame. The candle mirrors the intertwining of the Sabbath day with the rest of the days of the week. Finally, a blessing is said praising God for helping us to distinguish between various things in our lives, particularly the holy and the secular. The wine is sipped and then the candle is extinguished in the wine. People wish each other a "good week" and then return to their daily activities, which have been postponed for the Sabbath.

CHRISTIAN PARALLELS TO JEWISH SHABBAT OBSERVANCES

The Sabbath in Christian tradition has much in common with Jewish observance. While the modern Christian church does not typically follow the minutely detailed set of Shabbat prohibitions, traditionally Christians also did not work or do anything frivolous, such as going to the movies, on Sunday (the day that most Christians associate with the Sabbath). This tradition was reflected in the local "blue laws" in the United States, designed to keep most stores closed on Sunday. Mark Twain once joked, "The day was as long as a Protestant Sunday." During the Sabbath day, a Christian's goal was similar to a Jew's: to set aside time for meditation, to enjoy refreshment, and to spend time with family. Pressure from popular culture has placed many church services in conflict with civic groups, sports practices, and other diversions on Sunday morning. Recently, though, Christians have been rediscovering the importance of keeping the Sabbath for their spiritual health.

One aspect of the Sabbath where Judaism and much of Christianity have parted ways is on what day Shabbat should be observed. The Catholic Church and most Protestant churches observe the Sabbath on Sunday in commemoration of the resurrection of Jesus, which, according to the Gospels, happened on the first day of the week; that is, on Sunday. Some Christians, however, such as Seventh-Day Adventists, cite passages such as Acts 18:4, which says that Paul went to synagogue every Sabbath, to claim that the Saturday Sabbath was observed by Paul and should therefore still be observed on that day.

The difference between the observance of Sabbath days has historically caused difficulties for Jews economically. If Jews observed the Sabbath on Saturday and worked for a non-Jewish employer, there was tremendous pressure to work on Shabbat. This led to the radical suggestion by some nineteenth-century Reform rabbis in Germany to move the Jewish Sabbath to Sunday, to allow Jews to observe Shabbat without being pressured economically. In America, some rabbis in the late nineteenth century called for a five-day workweek, precisely so both Jews and Christians could observe their respective Sabbath days. As America moves to a seven-day week of commerce, with stores open every day, both faiths now suffer from the incessant call of commercialism.

A Final Note to the Reader

Rabbi Abraham Joshua Heschel, one of the preeminent rabbis of the latter half of the twentieth century, wrote the following regarding Jewish-Christian relations:

> We must insist upon loyalty to the unique and holy treasures of our own tradition and at the same time acknowledge that in this eon religious diversity may be the providence of God. Respect for each other's commitment, respect for each other's faith, is more than a political and social imperative. It is born of the insight that God is greater than religion, that faith is deeper than dogma, that theology has its roots in depth theology.[1]

This book and the work that we do to create bridges of understanding between the Jewish and Christian communities is born out of Rabbi Heschel's belief that religious diversity is the providence of God.

Rabbi Heschel was once asked if the world would in fact be better if it comprised just one religion, the logic being that there would be no religious strife. He responded negatively. Imagine, he implored his questioner, if every painting in the Metropolitan Museum looked the same. It is ludicrous, but so is the idea that there should only be one religion. "As far as I can tell," Rabbi Heschel wrote, "I think it is God's will that there should be religious pluralism."[2]

In some ways, this simple book is meant to be a guide to the painting of Judaism. When you are staring at a painting in a museum, you might enjoy it even if you are not familiar with the artist or the context of the painting. But much of the nuance and the richness of the art will be completely lost. This book, and the other books in the *A Brief Introduction for Christians* series from Jewish Lights Publishing, are meant to help explain the richness, the subtleties, and the meaning of the Jewish painting—so everyone can understand and enjoy them.

As Rabbi Heschel suggests, we believe that each of the religions of this world are different portraits of the One who gives life to all the painters. While the Jewish painting is one of the oldest, some of its most significant features are the layers of paint that have been added to the original. Even today, the Jewish painting continues to get "touched up" by new holidays and new rituals. We see this as part of the complex beauty of the Jewish way.

We hope that this book was helpful to you in deepening your understanding of Judaism and its development. We are optimistic that now, when you stand before the Jewish painting, you will view it with a deeper sensitivity and openness to its rich details. And in the process we pray that it will lead us all to a better world.

Jewish Holidays
Throughout the Year

Rosh Hashanah: September/October. Jewish New Year. Blow the ram's horn (shofar) in synagogue. Eat apples dipped in honey to symbolize a sweet year.

Yom Kippur: September/October. Day of Atonement. Following a period of introspection, reconcile with neighbors and friends. Fast and pray for forgiveness of the prior year's sins.

Sukkot: September/October. Commemorate the Israelites who wandered in the Sinai desert for forty years after the Exodus (see Passover). Build a backyard *sukkah* to replicate the movable huts in which they lived.

Simchat Torah: September/October. Complete the annual reading of the Torah (the Five Books of Moses) after reviewing a portion each week. Sing and parade around the synagogue.

Hanukkah: November/December. Celebrate the miraculous Judean triumph led by the Maccabee brothers over Assyrian-Greek religious persecution, ca. 164 BCE. Light the menorah, a candleholder for nine candles (one added each of eight nights, plus one to light the rest). Play dreidel (spinning top game) and eat latkes (potato pancakes).

Tu B'Shevat: End of January/February. Jewish earth day, the birthday of the trees. Give thanks for trees and eat fruit native to Israel in appreciation of the harvest.

Purim: End of February/March. Read the *megillah,* the story of Esther, who helped rescue the Jews of Persia from destruction by the king's evil advisor Haman, ca. 356 BCE. Children dress in costume and all present spin *groggers* (noisemakers) when Haman's name is mentioned. Adults celebrate with excessive spirits, encouraged on this festival only.

Passover/Pesach: April. Attend a seder ("ordered") meal to retell the Exodus story of Moses leading the Israelites from Egypt, ca. 1250 BCE. Celebrate deliverance from slavery to freedom, but remember those hard times by eating matzah (unleavened bread) and bitter herbs.

Yom Hashoah: April/May. Holocaust Remembrance Day. Solemnly memorialize the six million Jewish men, women, and children murdered by the Nazis, 1933–1945. Help ensure "Never Again."

Yom Hazikaron: April/May. Israeli Memorial Day. Mourn and honor the Israeli soldiers killed in defense of the Jewish homeland.

Yom Ha'atzmaut: April/May. Israeli Independence Day. Commemorates the declaration by David Ben-Gurion on May 14, 1948 of the birth of a modern Jewish state in formerly British-controlled Palestine, ending two thousand years without a sovereign Jewish country.

Lag B'Omer: April/May. Suspend for one day the mourning period between Passover and Shavuot called the "counting of the *Omer*," which originated as an agricultural tradition but became associated with tragic memories.

Shavuot: May/June. Commemorate the "covenant" made between God and the Jewish people with the giving of the Ten Commandments and the Torah on Mount Sinai. Decorate with flowers, eat dairy products, and stay up all night studying Torah.

Tisha B'Av: July/August. Fast and mourn the destruction of the First and Second Temples, and other tragedies of Jewish history associated with this date, the ninth day of the Hebrew month of Av.

Shabbat: Weekly, beginning at sunset on Friday night and ending roughly twenty-five hours later on Saturday. Shabbat is observed in numerous ways, but tradition calls for a time of rest and synagogue attendance and the reading of the weekly Torah portion in the synagogue.

HEBREW MONTH	SECULAR MONTH	JEWISH HOLIDAY
Nisan	March–April	Passover
Iyar	April–May	Yom Hashoah Yom Hazikaron Yom Ha'atzmaut Lag B'Omer
Sivan	May–June	Shavuot
Tammuz	June–July	Preparation for Tisha B'Av
Av	July–August	Tisha B'Av
Elul	August–September	Preparation for the High Holidays
Tishri	September–October	Rosh Hashanah Yom Kippur Sukkot Simchat Torah
Heshvan	October–November	None
Kislev	November–December	Hanukkah
Tevet	December–January	None
Shevat	January–February	Tu B'Shevat
Adar	February–March	Purim

THE FOUR MAJOR MOVEMENTS IN AMERICAN JUDAISM

There are four main Jewish religious movements in the United States and Canada. However, individual synagogues vary a great deal in their style and approach, particularly when it comes to worship, even among synagogues of the same movement. No movement is "one size fits all."

Reform

With roots in Germany, the Reform movement is the largest and oldest synagogue movement in North America, having been established in the nineteenth century. What sets it apart from the other movements is its contention that Jewish law is not divine in origin—that is, that the Torah was not revealed to the Jewish people on Mount Sinai at a specific time. Rather, it was written by human beings with divine inspiration. Thus the rules and practices of Judaism may be modified based on human judgment. As a result, members of the Reform movement represent a wide diversity in practice. The primary focus of the movement is on its affirmation of personal autonomy. Such personal decision-making when it comes to ritual and practice often leads individuals to choose to forgo rituals and practices that do not reflect contemporary mores and values. On a national level, direction for the movement is equally divided between rabbis, congregations, and the movement's rabbinical training seminary, Hebrew Union College–Jewish Institute of Religion (HUC–JIR).

Reform ideology rejects the classic Jewish notions of resurrection of the body in the afterlife and the idea of a personal messiah. On the social front, the Reform movement was an early champion of women's equality in Judaism, ordaining the first woman in the United States as a rabbi (Sally Priesand) at Hebrew Union College–Jewish Institute of Religion. Taking its cue from the Hebrew prophets, the movement has always been a strong advocate of social justice and social action to make society better.

Conservative

The Conservative movement was developed as a reaction to early and often controversial decisions and practices of the Reform movement, primarily in the early years of the twentieth century. Therefore, it is the second oldest American Jewish religious movement. It traces its roots to the historical school of Judaism in Europe. This school of thought attempted to stem the tide of assimilation brought on by the Enlightenment by applying the tools of history to the study of traditional Judaism and its practices. It maintained a strong commitment to Jewish nationhood, the Land of Israel, and the Hebrew language. It sought to *conserve* Judaism in the modern context.

The Conservative movement is a seminary-led movement, with the Jewish Theological Seminary at the helm. The law committee of its rabbinical organization (the Standards and Laws Committee of the Rabbinical Assembly) shapes the decisions for observance as it carefully walks the difficult path between tradition and modernity. Since it does not reject the binding nature of Jewish law but is also cognizant of the challenges of the contemporary world, it seeks to strike a feasible balance between the two. Unlike the Reform movement, it hesitates to draw sharp ideological lines between itself and the other movements.

Reconstructionist

This movement is the smallest and youngest, but it is growing quickly. While it might be considered to have grown out of the Conservative movement, it influences all the other movements as a result of the impact of the ideas of its founder, Rabbi Mordechai Kaplan. Its seminal synagogue institution, the Society for the Advancement of Judaism, was founded in New York City in 1922, but the Reconstructionist Federation was not founded until 1955. Kaplan sought to apply social science and Western democratic values to Judaism and *reconstruct* it in the process. He saw Judaism as an evolving civilization, not only a religion. The movement is socially progressive: Reconstructionist leaders were early champions of women's and gay rights within the Jewish community.

Borrowing from social theory, the Reconstructionist movement asserts that the decisions of the community take precedence over the decisions of the individual. Like the Reform movement, it rejects the traditional notion of the revelation of Torah at Mount Sinai. Reconstructionism also rejects the notion of a personal God who can intervene supernaturally in the world. Instead, it sees contemporary Judaism as the evolving result of the adaptation of Jewish religion and culture as it traveled through history from place to place. The movement does not see Jewish practices as the commandments of God. Rather, they are considered precious expressions of the past, part of the historical context in which they originated. While these Jewish traditions are treasured, it is the responsibility of each generation as a community—rather than as individuals—to evaluate such traditions and measure their value for the contemporary community. The Jewish people become the most important variable in such a reconstruction of Judaism. Reconstructionist Jews have always been advocates for the State of Israel, even as they have been strong advocates for America.

Orthodox

This is the modern designation for the part of the Jewish community that is most traditional and whose decisions are based strictly on Jewish law. The perspective of Orthodoxy is that this law was given to the Jewish people by God on Mount Sinai. The term *Orthodoxy* is borrowed from the Christian community and was used first by Reform Jews in the nineteenth century to refer to those who remained faithful to the practices and customs it was questioning. While there had been a range of practices in traditional Judaism up to the Middle Ages, Orthodoxy became quite fixed following the issuance of the first law codes during the medieval period. Nevertheless, there remains a great deal of diversity within the Orthodox community. From the outside it looks like there is little contemporary flexibility in practice among Orthodox Jews, but they too are struggling to react positively within their own parameters to various aspects of modernity, such as the rights of women. Orthodoxy as a movement might be said to represent a continuum of Orthodox groups that includes those far to the right, such as the so-called settlers' movement in Israel as well as various communities of Hasidim and those liberal Orthodox groups that refer to themselves as centrists.

Orthodoxy rejects the so-called progressive revelation, which is a tenet of Reform Judaism. It also denies most forms of historical criticism of sacred text. In the synagogue one of the most salient features is that men and women do not sit together in prayer.

NOTES

CHAPTER 1: ROSH HASHANAH/NEW YEAR

1. Quoted in S. Y. Agnon, *Days of Awe* (New York: Schocken Books, 1975), p. xi.
2. *Midrash Tehillim* 27:4.
3. Quoted in Martin Buber, *Tales of the Hasidim* (New York: Schocken Books, 1975), p. 64.

CHAPTER 2: YOM KIPPUR/DAY OF ATONEMENT

1. Abraham Joshua Heschel, *The Sabbath* (New York: Farrar, Straus & Giroux, 1975), p. 10.
2. Quoted in Nahum Glatzer, *Franz Rosenzweig: His Life and Thought* (New York: Schocken Books, 1953), p. 333.
3. Moses Maimonides, *Hilkhot Teshuvah* 2:1.
4. Quoted in Agnon, *Days of Awe,* p. x.

CHAPTER 7: PESACH/PASSOVER

1. The whole story appears in *Like Bread on the Seder Plate: Jewish Lesbians and the Transformation of Tradition* by Rabbi Rebecca Alpert (New York: Columbia University Press, 1998).

A FINAL NOTE TO THE READER

1. Abraham Joshua Heschel, "What Ecumenism Is," in *Moral Grandeur and Spiritual Audacity*, ed. Susannah Heschel (New York: Farrar, Straus and Giroux, 1996), p. 287.
2. Ibid., p. 403.

GLOSSARY

afikoman (pronounced a-fee-KO-min): based on a Greek word meaning "after procession," used to describe a special piece of matzah hidden away near the beginning of the seder by one of the adults, and searched for toward the end of the seder by the children.

akdamut (pronounced ahk-da-MOOT): eleventh-century liturgical poem read during the morning service of the first day of Shavuot.

aliyah (pronounced ah-lee-YAH): "going up," to the Torah for its reading; a blessing is recited before and after the reading. This is also the term used for immigration to Israel ("making *aliyah*").

challah (pronounced KHAH-lah): special twisted or braided egg bread that is used on the Sabbath and holidays.

chametz (pronounced khah-MAYTZ): food that is prohibited to eat or even to own on Passover.

charoset (pronounced khah-RO-set): a mix of apples, raisins, and wine eaten on Passover to symbolize the mortar used by Israelite slaves.

chatan bereshit (pronounced khah-TAN bi-ray-SHEET): "Genesis groom"; honor given to the second individual called to the honor of the Torah on Simchat Torah.

chatan Torah (pronounced khah-TAN to-RAH): "Torah groom"; honor given to the first individual called to the honor of the Torah on Simchat Torah.

dreidel (pronounced DRAY-dil): spinning top used for Hanukkah game.

etrog (pronounced EH-trohg): citron used on Sukkot.

gelt (pronounced gelt): Yiddish for "money," especially given on Hanukkah.

grogger (pronounced GRAH-ger): Yiddish for Purim noise-maker; *raashan* in Hebrew.

hakafot (pronounced hah-kah-FOHT): Torah processionals.

halakhah (pronounced hah-lah-KHAH): the "way to walk"; Jewish law.

Hallel Psalms (pronounced HAH-lel): Psalms 113–118.

hamantaschen (pronounced khah-men-TAH-shen): pastry pockets that are eaten on Purim.

hanukkiyah (pronounced khah-noo-KEE-ah): Hanukkah menorah or candleholder.

Hasidism (pronounced kha-SEE-dism): a religious movement, begun in the seventeenth century, that emphasizes joy and God's nearness.

Havdalah (pronounced havh-dah-LAH): brief ritual ceremony that marks the transition between the Sabbath and the rest of the week.

Hol Hamoed (pronounced CHOL hah-mo-ED): intermediate days of a festival.

Jew-by-choice: a modern term used to refer to converts to Judaism; generally considered to be a more sensitive and embracing term than *convert*.

kaparah (pronounced kah-pah-RAH): a ritual slaughtering of a chicken as atonement for sins; practiced by a small group of Orthodox Jews as part of Yom Kippur observance.

ketubah (pronounced kih-TOO-bah): wedding contract.

Kiddush (pronounced KIH-dush): from the word for "holy" or "separate"; blessing said over wine that introduces the Sabbath and holidays.

kittel (pronounced KIH-tel): burial shroud worn during Yom Kippur to remind us of our mortality.

Kol Nidre (pronounced KOL nee-DRAY): Yom Kippur prayer releasing one from vows to be taken in the coming year.

latkes (pronounced LAHT-kes): potato pancakes fried in oil and eaten on Hanukkah.

lulav (pronounced loo-LAHV): palm branch used on Sukkot.

maror (pronounced mah-ROAR): bitter herbs eaten on Passover to symbolize the bitterness of slavery.

matzah (pronounced mah-TZAH): unleavened bread eaten on Passover.

Megillat Esther (pronounced mih-GEE-laht ES-ter): the scroll of Esther read on Purim, often referred to just as the *megillah,* although there are other biblical books (Ruth, Song of Songs, Ecclesiastes, and Lamentations) that are written on scrolls.

menorah (pronounced mih-NO-rah): candelabra or candle-holder, generally used on Shabbat and Hanukkah but also in the ancient Temple in Jerusalem.

mikvah (pronounced mik-VAH): ritual bath.

mishloach manot (pronounced meesh-LOH-akh mah-NOHT): tradition of giving baskets of fruits and pastries to friends on Purim.

mitzvot (pronounced MEETZ-voht): commandments, plural of mitzvah.

Omer (pronounced OH-mer): period of counting from the second night of Passover until Shavuot.

persumat ha'nes (pronounced peer-SOO-mat hah-NAYS): "making known the miracle"; usually associated with the lighting of the candles on Hanukkah in a place that can be seen.

Purimshpiels (pronounced POOR-im-shpeels): spoofs that tell the Purim story and make fun of local religious leaders.

seder (pronounced SAY-der): from the word "order"; refers to the orderly Passover meal that takes place on the first two nights of Passover.

Selichot (pronounced si-lee-KHOHT): penitential prayers recited in the days before Yom Kippur.

Shabbat (pronounced shah-BAHT): the Jewish Sabbath day, which begins at sunset on Friday.

shalosh regalim (pronounced shah-LOHSH reh-gah-LEEM): the three pilgrimage holidays mentioned in the Bible— Passover, Shavuot, and Sukkot.

shammash (pronounced shah-MAHSH): helper candle used to light other Hanukkah candles.

Shema (pronounced shih-MAH): creedal prayer of Judaism, recited twice daily.

shofar (pronounced shoh-FAR): ram's horn blown on Rosh Hashanah.

sufganiot (pronounced soof-gah-nee-YOT): jelly doughnuts eaten on Hanukkah.

taanit Esther (pronounced tah-ah-NEET ES-ter): the "fast of Esther," which takes place the day before Purim.

tallit (pronounced tah-LEET): prayer shawl.

tashlikh (pronounced tash-LEEKH): casting of bread crumbs that symbolize sins into water on Rosh Hashanah.

teshuvah (pronounced tih-SHOO-vah): repentance done during Rosh Hashanah and Yom Kippur.

tikkun layl Shavuot (pronounced Tee-KOON LAYL shah-voo-OT): all-night study session on Shavuot.

tractate: divisions, or major sections (larger than a chapter), of the Talmud, which are named according to their primary theme and then further subdivided.

trope (pronounced trop): system of musical cantillation notes for the public chanting of the Torah and other selections of the Bible; called *taamei hamikrah* in Hebrew.

Unetaneh Tokef (pronounced oo-neh-TAH-neh TOH-kef): "Let us proclaim"; central prayer of the High Holidays.

Yamim Noraim (pronounced yah-MEEM no-rah-EEM): the "Days of Awe"; the days between Rosh Hashanah and Yom Kippur.

Yizkor (pronounced yiz-KOHR): memorial service.

Zohar (pronounced ZOH-har): primary source for Jewish mysticism.

Suggestions for Further Reading

Anisfeld, Sharon Cohen, Tara Mohr, and Catherine Spector, eds. *The Women's Passover Companion: Women's Reflections on the Festival of Freedom*. Woodstock, Vt.: Jewish Lights Publishing, 2006.

————. *The Women's Seder Sourcebook: Rituals and Readings for Use at the Passover Seder*. Woodstock, Vt.: Jewish Lights Publishing, 2006.

Elkins, Dov Peretz. *Rosh Hashanah Readings: Inspiration, Information and Contemplation*. Woodstock, Vt.: Jewish Lights Publishing, 2006.

————. *Yom Kippur Readings: Inspiration, Information and Contemplation*. Woodstock, Vt.: Jewish Lights Publishing, 2005.

Frankiel, Tamar. *Kabbalah: A Brief Introduction for Christians*. Woodstock, Vt.: Jewish Lights Publishing, 2006.

Gillman, Neil. *The Jewish Approach to God: A Brief Introduction for Christians*. Woodstock, Vt.: Jewish Lights Publishing, 2003.

Greenberg, Irving. *The Jewish Way: Living the Holidays*. New York: Summit Books, 1988.

Kula, Irwin, and Vanessa Ochs. *The Book of Jewish Sacred Practices: CLAL's Guide to Everyday and Holiday Rituals and Blessings*. Woodstock, Vt.: Jewish Lights Publishing, 2001.

Kushner, Lawrence. *Jewish Spirituality: A Brief Introduction for Christians.* Woodstock, Vt.: Jewish Lights Publishing, 2001.

Olitzky, Kerry M., and Ronald Isaacs. *The Complete "How to" Handbook for Jewish Living.* Hoboken, N.J.: KTAV, 2004.

Olitzky, Kerry M., and Dan Judson. *Jewish Ritual: A Brief Introduction for Christians.* Woodstock, Vt.: Jewish Lights Publishing, 2004.

Wolfson, Ron. *Hanukkah: The Family Guide to Spiritual Celebration,* 2nd ed. Woodstock, Vt.: Jewish Lights Publishing, 2001.

———. *Passover: The Family Guide to Spiritual Celebration,* 2nd ed. Woodstock, Vt.: Jewish Lights Publishing, 2003.

———. *Shabbat: The Family Guide to Preparing for and Celebrating the Sabbath,* 2nd ed. Woodstock, Vt.: Jewish Lights Publishing, 2002.

About Jewish Lights

People of all faiths and backgrounds yearn for books that attract, engage, educate, and spiritually inspire.

Our principal goal is to stimulate thought and help all people learn about who the Jewish People are, where they come from, and what the future can be made to hold. While people of our diverse Jewish heritage are the primary audience, our books speak to people in the Christian world as well and will broaden their understanding of Judaism and the roots of their own faith.

We bring to you authors who are at the forefront of spiritual thought and experience. While each has something different to say, they all say it in a voice that you can hear.

Our books are designed to welcome you and then to engage, stimulate, and inspire. We judge our success not only by whether or not our books are beautiful and commercially successful, but by whether or not they make a difference in your life.

For your information and convenience, at the back of this book we have provided a list of other Jewish Lights books you might find interesting and useful. They cover all the categories of your life:

Bar/Bat Mitzvah
Bible Study / Midrash
Children's Books
Congregation Resources
Current Events / History
Ecology / Environment
Fiction: Mystery, Science Fiction
Grief / Healing
Holidays / Holy Days
Inspiration
Kabbalah / Mysticism / Enneagram

Life Cycle
Meditation
Men's Interest
Parenting
Prayer / Ritual / Sacred Practice
Social Justice
Spirituality
Theology / Philosophy
Travel
Twelve Steps
Women's Interest

Printed in the USA
CPSIA information can be obtained
at www.ICGtesting.com
JSHW082209140824
68134JS00014B/521

9 781580 233026